EUGENIA PRICE

Woman to Woman

Zondervan Books
Zondervan Publishing House
Grand Rapids, Michigan

Turner Publishing Company
Nashville, Tennessee
www.turnerpublishing.com

Woman to Woman

Cover design: Bruce Gore

Library of Congress Cataloging-in-Publication Data Upon Request

9781684425747   paperback
9781684425754   hardback
97816

17 18 19 20 10 9 8 7 6 5 4 3 2 1

To My Mother
Who is showing me more and more
the value of a Christ-controlled personality.

PREFACE

I have written this book after several years of gradual, though sometimes staggering, realizations about women!

Being one, we have always interested me. Now, however, I stand in awe of my own sex. Not because we are such a magnificent lot, but because God has placed such breathtaking responsibility in our hands. He has placed human lives in our hands. And to Him these are His dearest possessions. For some reason known only to Him, He has created into woman a frightening ability to leave marks on these lives which are so dear to Him.

A woman attempting to live her life with her own personality entirely in her own hands, can be a monster loosed. A woman living her life with her personality in the hands of Christ, can be a sure, creative benediction.

Woman to Woman is an informally written book. I have simply "let down my hair" with you and shared some of what Christ has taught me in my own life and through the lives of other women with whom I have come in contact. I have tried to show the altogether amazing difference it makes whether or not a woman's life is Christ-controlled. I have tried to be practical. I have spattered the pages with true stories, some glorious, some tragic. But they are all stories which you will recognize and they are built around problems which you will know.

Almost four years have been spent gathering the material and the realizations which I have shared here. Nothing has been included which I have not known to work in a woman's life. I suggest that you look carefully at the table of contents and you will see that the following chapters cover the potential trouble areas in a woman's life all the way from her disposition to the way she faces death.

In the one instance where I have asked that you reread certain chapters, please take time to do it. The Christian life is a *whole,* and it has not been simple to break it up into chapters. And although I have written it informally—woman to woman —I hope you will concentrate as you read.

I must warmly thank all those who knowingly or unknowingly helped me gather the material for *Woman to Woman.* The teenagers and their mothers. The letters which have come. My thanks also to my associate, Rosalind Rinker, for her great help in sorting and arranging the material, and for her prayers and daily encouragement as I wrote. From my heart, I thank all of you who prayed for me. Lillian Lubbert, as always, handled the typing of my manuscript with love and care, and being married, kept me well encouraged on my chapters on family life.

As I have written, I have prayed daily that you who read it, will close the book—each one of you, with a Christ-controlled life.

EUGENIA PRICE

Chicago, Illinois
June, 1959

CONTENTS

CONTENTS

1

The Difference It Makes When a
Woman's Personality
Is Christ-controlled

1

The Difference It Makes When a Woman's Personality Is Christ-controlled

We women are blamed for many things which we do not do.

We women are praised for being what we certainly are not. Mothers are extolled in the wordy stanzas of the Mother's Day greeting card versifiers as being so nearly perfect no one but God could possibly live up to them!

When mother love is of the quality God intended it to be, it *is* probably closest to the love of God of all the kinds of human love which exist. But, it is a little considered fact that simply in the process of becoming a mother, one does not automatically become a saint.

Over and over, as I travel about the country and speak woman to woman, with women in all walks of life, I hear the wail, "Why are we blamed for everything that goes wrong with our children? We're doing the best we know to do. Why doesn't someone tell us *how* to anticipate our teenagers instead of pointing out, when the damage is done, what we did that was wrong? Isn't it ever just a little bit someone else's fault? Are we always to blame?"

Over and over, as I talk with women riding to or from an airport or a train station in their cars, or over coffee in their living rooms at night after my meetings, I have been given intimate glimpses into their troubled hearts. Actually most of them are not reading what today's psychologists are saying about parent-teen or husband-wife relationships. Some are, it is true, but Christian women especially seem to believe that it's up to God to handle everything. And when things go wrong, they follow the familiar pattern of self-pity. There are always restful exceptions. Now and then I find a woman who has enough elasticity of soul to say simply that she knows she has fallen down somewhere along the line. In these women I sense an almost unconscious knowledge that God made women in such a way that they wield a singular kind of mysterious influence over the lives their lives touch.

The women with whom I have honest conversation are not only married women with children's and husband's lives in their hands. Being a single woman myself, hundreds of unmarried women and widows have poured out their lonely, puzzled, otherwise locked-up hearts to me. God created them in exactly the same way He created married women, with the same desires, the same needs and the same deadly or blessed weapon of womanly influence.

As we move through the pages of this book we will share some of these conversations, some of them carried on by mail with women whom I shall never meet on this earth, but whose hearts and minds are just like mine. Just like yours. Woman hearts. Woman minds. Created by God in the special way He created women.

I have Scriptural backing for this statement that God created into woman a particular power to influence. Not many days before I began the writing of this book, I was talking with Dr. Wilbur M. Smith of Fuller Theological Seminary. As we discussed my book, he wisely showed me that God backed up my thinking in the Book of Genesis. In the otherwise tightly written narrative of chapter three which tells of our first parents in the Garden of Eden, almost six complete verses are given over to the first attack by the tempter on the first woman. The wily one went straight to Eve, and the entire basic problem of human nature, the right to one's self, sprang into being through a woman! He didn't approach Adam. He approached Eve. In the sixth verse of Genesis three, there is a mention of Eve's husband. A mere fragment which says, ". . . he did eat." That's all there is in God's written down Word about Eve's husband and the first temptation.

This does not in any way minimize man. It merely points up the deadly impact of woman. And right now, it is important for us to see that this God-given influence of woman is no virtue at all. In itself it is neutral, neither good nor bad. It is what we do with it that matters. But after years of contact with women of all backgrounds and personality types, I am convinced that most of us are not aware of the power of this innate ability to mark the lives of those whose lives we touch.

I have passed through varying stages of blaming women, of defending them, of criticizing and condoning. None of this is valid. *Understanding* of ourselves must come first. And until I reached the place where I feel I am identified with womankind, not by experience, but by grace, I would not have dared write this book.

I am now convinced that no woman means to scar the lives of those around her. I am now convinced that most women are in darkness on this point. I am now convinced of their own heartaches when their loved ones are damaged and the fact that the women themselves might have acted differently has just not occurred to them. I have been speaking plainly along these lines now for four years. As I write, a note which was sent to me after a women's retreat in California, comes to my mind. The note was written by a lovely Christian woman who had, I'm sure, always done what she honestly saw to be right. But her children had turned away from God. Mother's religion bored them. The Holy Spirit had spoken to her during this retreat and she had heard. The note was written with poignant openness and honesty. "Genie, what can I do now? Suddenly, after years and years, I see I have been so self-righteous in my Christianity that I have driven my family away from God!"

Up to that moment, this woman had been in darkness on this point. Sincerity is *not* enough. We need the very sensitivity of God Himself in order to live lives which mark with beauty the other lives we influence. If we use only our own sincerity and religious convictions, we will surely scar with ugliness. To the average good, moral church woman the word ugliness is too much to face. Especially when it is applied to something she has done.

But we belong to a Redeemer God, and it is never too late for Him to redeem anything! How much better to see, even if the seeing means humiliating exposure of our stupidity or lack of perception.

Let's face it, a woman's influence is perhaps no more important than a man's influence, but it *is* different. Women scar hearts and souls. God did not give us this power to influence without a reason. But it is certain that He did give it to us. Not to use as Eve used hers over Adam. This was the very moment sin entered the world and infected all human nature. And we are being unrealistic and hiding behind the long touted and utterly false "weak little woman" theory when we refuse to admit that sin entered the world through a woman; when we refuse to admit that it invaded the human race through a woman's influence!

". . . he did eat." Adam ate because Eve talked him into it.

I began facing these facts toward the end of the five year period in my own life during which I had written and directed a dramatic radio series called "Unshackled." The series told true stories of men and women whose lives had been restored to wholeness through a personal encounter with Jesus Christ. I believe I wrote over two hundred and fifty scripts. I interviewed most of the persons myself. And one day I did some counting. Two hundred and twelve of these two hundred and fifty men or women had been directly twisted or blessed by the influence of a woman. And the woman who blessed or scarred the lives was not always the mother either. Often she was a school teacher, a sweetheart, a wife, a daughter, a grandmother, an aunt. But in two hundred and twelve instances out of two hundred and fifty the most influential person had been a woman!

I am sorry to report that in most cases the woman's influence was destructive. Gladly I remember the stories in which the woman's touch was a good, creative touch. But they were in the minority. Be that as it may, for now we are facing merely the *impact* of women. We are not all strong characters who noticeably dominate. Often a woman who is weak and sorry for herself and timid to a point of high egocentricity, can leave the deepest scars upon the lives around her. Extreme timidity is not humility. It is often neurotic self-consciousness and self-love. A weepy woman who has to be protected from life can twist the lives of her loved ones to an appalling degree.

Whatever the personality type, the basic fact remains: Women hold within their natures a potentially dangerous power to mark lives. All women. Married and single. Thin and fat. Tall and short. Educated and uneducated. Weak and strong. Shrinking violets and domineering frigates in full sail.

I have no way of knowing what Christianity means to you who read this book. To me it means that I have at last found out that I am not able to cope with life. This is not a sign of weakness. It is, according to the Bible, simply being realistic about human nature. "All have sinned and come short of the glory of God." But it means something more. It means that I have clearly seen my need of a Saviour. I do not believe this in order that I will be considered a fundamentally sound Christian. It has nothing whatever to do with the fact that I want to be known as holding the correct Biblical doctrine. Correct Biblical doctrine is simply an explanation of things as they are.

There is nothing more destructive than a tight-lipped Christian woman whose attitude exposes her refusal to accept God's Word, while she loudly and heatedly dresses down someone who doesn't hold with her doctrinal emphasis! A Christian is the last person who should feel impelled to prove herself right. A true Christian is one who *knows* her need to be made right. And an attitude of belligerence or scorn at anything cuts directly across the deepest meaning of Calvary. Christians whose lives are working are those who have relaxed in the self-effort department. Those who have seen at last that in themselves is no good thing. *But* who have also seen that with those selves eternally linked with the life of Christ, the human personality potential is glorious. We have all fallen short of the glory of God within ourselves. This is no insult. This is fact. But God did not stop with this belittling statement about us. He did not even mean it to belittle. Just to clarify. *Then* He visited this earth in the Person of Jesus Christ and did something about the glorious possibilities which lie within each human personality. He knows all there is to know about the twisting, deforming power of sin. He coped with it Himself on the Cross. I don't understand how He did it, but I know He did it.

This then, is the lovely arrangement God has worked out. All the destructive power within us *can* be controlled by the very life of Christ. When we receive Him into our lives, He comes. And with Him comes all the magnificent potential of *not* falling short of the glory of God.

Woman's influence remains exactly the same in strength and power. If you are a Christian, your influence is no stronger than if you are not. But it can be under the personal control of Jesus Christ, "the express image of God." The areas of your personality which are under His control are going to wield a creative, positive influence. They have to, not because of what you are like, but because of what He is like. The areas not under His control will be the trouble areas. Human judgment and human love just do not extend far enough to avoid trouble. They are not infallible, even if they were elastic enough to extend themselves. He is infallible. He is God.

It must be remembered and admitted that there are times when we have acted directly under His control and influence, and trouble has still come. Sometimes it has brought with it an even greater human conflict. Sometimes the darkness is so thick we give up even trying to see our way out of it. *But* if we have acted under His control, then the total responsibility rests with Him!

We can just go on and wait for Him to do something about it.

The human personality completely under the control of Jesus Christ is responsible to Him. Not to the solution of the problem. The problem is His. On the Cross He assumed complete responsibility for the plight of the entire human race. A tragedy almost as great as the Cross itself is the tragedy of His followers refusing to let Him act on this tremendous responsibility.

There will be times when we misunderstand His intentions. When we mistake His guidance. When we quite sincerely do just the opposite of what He would have us do. I have found that the responsibility is still His. If I am honestly holding back nothing from His control, then He will go right on being

a Redeemer God, making oftentimes glorious creative use of
even my blunders and mistakes.

As we move from chapter to chapter, we will look at spe-
cific areas of a woman's life in which she is free to choose
whether she will be herself or let Him be Himself in her.

Your trouble may lie in the fact that you are a Stoic at
heart. You may quite unknowingly be depriving yourself of
God's best for you by making use of your own will power and
calling it Christianity. You may be right in your thinking, but
if you are in control of your own personality, the stronger
your will, the redder will become your face as you hammer
your opinions mercilessly into the personalities of those you
love.

Your trouble may be whimpering self-pity. Tears are said
to become a woman, and so we let them flow luxuriously. And
we often love to talk about our beloved symptoms. I take argument with those who say women are sorrier for themselves
than men. Self-pity is believed to be the basis of most alcohol-
ism and after all, though we are catching up with them, there
are still more male alcoholics in the world. So, I do not believe
us to be any more guilty of self-pity than men. But we do
make more use of it! We let it be known.

Thousands of women with problems fall into the strong-
hearted Stoic or the whimpering self-pitying class. But there
are still more thousands in between. Just women. We can
only gain from this book if we are completely honest with
ourselves and with God. Perhaps now would be the time for
us to take grace and then take a good look at ourselves.

Do you classify yourself as a strong-willed Stoic who depends upon herself first? Do you classify yourself as a woman
who is, however unconsciously, making a career of feeling
sorry for herself?

Or are you in the majority group in between?

Are you neither a Stoic with great human courage nor a

chronic complainer? Are you just one of the rest of us for whom life's troubles often overflow their bounds? Is your daily routine wearing you down and does mealtime seem to come six times a day instead of three? Do you have to do a laundry every day and are there (some weeks at least) nine or ten days in your week instead of seven? Perhaps your heart is broken by some fresh grief and the pieces are getting lost one by one and there seems no hope for mending. Perhaps your prayer life is a dead thing and God seems to have stopped His ears to the sound of your voice. Maybe you're just so tired physically that you look longingly at every quiet, tree-shaded cemetery you pass. Or perhaps your body is wearing out and with it your interest in life. Maybe you're growing old in years and the very heart within you, which feels just the same as it did when you were eighteen, is crying out in helpless protest at the sag and the dim eyes and the failing memory. You may be so lonely you sometimes question the God who lets you keep on waking up every day to more loneliness. You may feel so useless you wonder why you were born in the first place. Or maybe you bear the scorching humiliation of knowing that you are a burden to someone. Maybe you're no longer sure of anyone's love. No mail in the box. No sound from the telephone. Nothing. Perhaps your life is too filled with nothing. Your mother's heart may ache and tremble with fear for one of your children. You may be wincing under the sharpest of all pain for a woman—jealousy. Perhaps you've imagined your husband is looking at another woman. Perhaps he really is. The agony of jealousy is just as sharp in either case.

Your problem could be you. It could be a member of your family. It could be that you have no family at all. Whatever it is, He knows about it. Whatever it is, if you have had it a while and are still troubled by it, you should see by now that you can't cope with it.

But Christ can.

He *is* one and the same with God. Either He is, or He was mistaken about Himself because He said, "I and the Father are one."

Life is never going to be without trouble. "Man is born unto trouble, as the sparks fly upward." Jesus graciously reminded us that if we follow Him we will not be exempt from trouble. "In the world ye shall have tribulation: but be of good cheer; I have overcome the world."

What does He mean? I am not satisfied with theory. I demand to know, in my daily life, how I can learn to cope with my tribulations. I demand to know in what way He has overcome the world which is sometimes so troublesome to me. You have a right to demand it too. I will postulate no theories. We will look at facts. Actual situations in which all women find themselves. Find themselves helpless, over and over again.

Jesus Christ tells us quite clearly that we are to lose our lives for His sake. To me, this means that my total personality is to be placed into His hands, under His control.

If He is who He claims to be, then day by day, I have a right to expect that I will become influenced by Him. I have a right to expect that day by day, as I grow in the knowledge of Him, I will be more able to cope creatively with the various trouble areas in my life.

For the remainder of this book we will look at these actual trouble areas in the lives of women living in the middle twentieth century. And if we are honest, perhaps we will find the answer to the question. What difference does it make whether or not a woman's personality is Christ-controlled?

2

The Difference Christ Makes . . .

IN YOUR DISPOSITION

2

The Difference Christ Makes ...

IN YOUR DISPOSITION

One of the deepest of woman's instincts is to believe in her heart (no matter what she may say about it) that her disposition is her own! In other words, she has a right to it. In reality, a disposition is an outward thing. It is merely a manifestation of what is *inside*.

You are what your disposition shows you to be.

I am what my disposition shows me to be.

And because all women to some extent are actresses, this is one of the things which makes and keeps us such puzzling creatures where men are concerned. We seem to be one way and down inside we are capable of being entirely another. One of the most charming women I know gives every outward appearance of caring about other people. She does—from a pedestal. Because her acts of kindness are geared **to** seeing to it that others know how kind she really is. This does not diminish her social charm, except to the three or four persons nearest to her who have, at last, seen that here is true self-love seeming to pour itself out upon other people. But in the very acts of kindness, it is building its own esteem for it-self.

After many contacts with Christian women of all kinds in the past several years, I have almost stopped listening to their talk. Instead, I unroll a specially developed pair of antennae and begin to try to sense their true natures by what they *are*. Women talk well. By nature we are clever. There is Scriptural proof for this in the story of our sister, Eve. This is our in-herited nature. We are the world's most skillful rationalizers.

And in my sincere effort to make this a fair-minded book, I would say a word in defense of the men with whom God has seen fit to populate the planet earth. Usually it is the woman who is considered the most spiritual in a family. Not always, but usually. Nine times out of ten it is the woman who is "holding on in prayer" *and* "holding on" in conversation often to the point of dullness in behalf of her husband who is not as "spiritual" as he should be.

Often this is true. But often it is not true at all. The woman believes it to be true because by nature she is even clever enough to convince herself.

Several years ago a young man became a Christian during the time I was speaking in the community in which he lived. His wife did not. But a few months later, she did. Now her friends tell me she has gone ahead of her husband by leaps and bounds and he is standing still spiritually.

Why is this? Is it because women have a deeper spiritual capacity than men? In some instances, yes. But not in all. We dare not speak in generalities where the life of the Spirit is concerned. I have found out that the young wife, who fol-lowed her husband into the Kingdom of God a few months later, and who is said to have gone so far ahead of him spiritu-ally, is working hard in her church. This is good. She is keep-ing a daily quiet time. This is good. She is witnessing to her new found faith. Also good. But she is boasting about it! She is enjoying her success as a Christian. She is discussing her husband too often with her friends. They are all praying for him and perhaps without realizing it, are looking down their pretty, righteous noses at the poor fellow.

His wife's overpowering, extroverted disposition is swamping the boy. He is quiet and introverted by nature. He came thoughtfully and with great certainty into a personal relationship with Jesus Christ. He doesn't say a lot about it, he doesn't tell everyone (under the guise of witnessing!) that he never misses his quiet time. Maybe he does miss it. I'm sure he isn't perfect. But neither is he the same person as his wife.

His disposition is entirely different from hers. Personally, I would prefer his. But this couple may be heading for serious trouble simply because no one involved seems to have realized that when we become followers of Jesus Christ, He comes to indwell us. We have minute by minute access to His personality! And He respects individual differences among us. We speak a lot about respecting them, but we seldom react one to the other as though we had any reverence at all for the differences in human personalities. If both of these new Christians could see the tremendous potential of Christ's personality within them, things would change.

The quiet husband might relax his silence somewhat.

The talkative, busy-busy young wife might relax her "spiritual speed" and begin to discover that God's voice is a still small voice.

In this particular instance, it will have to be the woman who is changed first. Always, the most dominant personality causes the commotion. I have advised this woman to confess her over-activity to her quiet husband, to ask him to help her slow down and learn to be quiet. This should help release him. As things are now, he undoubtedly feels inferior to her spiritually. And the very fact that he became a Christian first probably only adds to his sense of inferiority with her.

I have no way of knowing, but I suspect that the man in question has a simpler, saner, deeper walk with Christ than his much-praying, much-witnessing, overly-enthusiastic wife.

No doubt she is saying quite sincerely (because she *is* sincere and well-intentioned), "But this is the way I am! I'm just a bubbler and I can't help it. My mother is like this." Or, "My father is like this."

Let us face the fact once and for all that when we are converted to Jesus Christ, we are reborn of God! We still retain characteristics and tendencies inherited from our human family. But we have become members of a new family. The family of God. Now we have access to a new inheritance. When we became Christians we "were born, not of blood, nor of the will of the flesh, nor of the will of man, but of God."

Daily I need to remind myself of this. I don't do it daily, but I should. I certainly need to be reminded. In fact, between the writing of the first and second chapters of this very book, I demonstrated my point perfectly. Most persons find it hard to believe that I am *not* extroverted by nature. When I tell them I love nothing in all the world as much as I love privacy and to be alone away from crowds, they look at me as though I am lying! But it is true. It is a sure Price family trait. Before I became a Christian and began to see that Christians really have no rights, I lived a (to me) lovely ivory tower existence. I saw only those who amused or pleased or interested or bettered me.

I have sincerely tried to submit this defect in my personality to Jesus Christ. As long as it is submitted, I get along very well. But almost invariably, when I begin to write a book, the old girl (as she really is) comes to life! For the first few days I struggle mightily with a self-defense that for a time overwhelms me. I rationalize with the most skillful of my sex: "After all, I haven't allowed enough time to write this book! I've taken too many speaking engagements again. I must not throw this book together. I must write it carefully. And it does seem as though God's people—all people—would find enough of even the old tired milk of human kindness in their hearts to leave me alone just long enough to do it!" I sigh every time the telephone rings. I cringe when the doorbell rings. I resent the daily stack of mail to be answered. I have written five books and this time I seemed to have a harder time than ever before. To all indications I am slipping horribly as a Christian.

But now that I have finally gone to the Lord with it minus pious phrases, I have seen that some of the reason, at least, is that this is the first book I have written since I have been sharing a house with my new associate, Rosalind Rinker. I had a new audience! Here was someone brand new to impress with the great need of a writer for solitude and aloneness. Of course, my disposition flared more than ever because I felt guilty underneath, knowing that she too has a book to write during the same months. But she has been a missionary all of her adult life and is well accustomed to interruptions. I've been a professional writer all of my adult life and I'm accustomed to proper writing conditions. More rationalization!

Yesterday I did nothing whatever on the book. The telephone, the mail, the window-washer, a new convert in trouble, a Christian with a genuine need of advice, missionary friends leaving for a foreign country, a board meeting to be scheduled and planned for, a dinner engagement I had to keep and on and on ad nauseam. Ad nauseam to me. All God's work and all tough on *my* disposition.

The fact that you are reading this book now is proof that it makes all the difference in the world whether or not a disposition is Christ-controlled! Today I have given mine back to Him. It seemed a rather ungracious gift on my part, but being as He is, He took it graciously. I am rested and I have stopped being the temperamental writer!

Being human, we blame either our heredity or our current circumstances for our dispositions. Both can be blamed. But if our entire personalities are under the control of Jesus Christ, we are *enabled* to act as He would act. Even with our heredity. Even with our current circumstances.

Not once in His earthly life do we find a record of easy circumstances. His human heredity was average. And yet, He met His daily round with poise and great inner calm. He was God controlled. He permitted Himself to be. According to the Bible, He was "in all points tempted like as we are." What a relief this is! But He, being One with God, kept Himself under control.

We cannot do this under all circumstances. But He can. He can keep us under control if we allow Him to do it. And every time we act under His control (when we would do something entirely different), I believe that something of His nature is added to ours. Something of Christ Himself is added to our inner selves. This inner self is what will be showing, don't forget, when we stand before Him one day stripped of our human bodies and our circumstantial alibis.

There is little sense in our complaining that He was God and could control Himself. This is not the point. Jesus Christ became utterly human, too. And it is imperative that we see *why* He was under heavenly control. Over and over we read in the New Testament that He came to do the will of His Father. His motives were unmixed.

I find that my disposition plays god (and havoc) in my life when my motives are *not* unmixed! I find during those times of half following Christ and half following myself, that I lack wisdom. Wise persons are always quiet, certain people. Have you ever noticed that? And truly wise human beings are those who dwell deep in God. Making use of His personality in them. Making use of His wisdom. If our motives are mixed motives, we lack His wisdom. It is contaminated with our own. James wrote a deep truth about human nature when he wrote, "A double minded man is unstable in all his ways." He is.

And our instability shows nowhere as flagrantly as it shows in our dispositions.

Men and women both excuse their dispositions on the grounds of heredity or circumstances. But I believe in all fairness that women have another excuse which is rather exclusively theirs. We don't put it into words. We don't admit it publicly. Usually we aren't even aware of it ourselves. But deep within our feminine personalities is the conviction that we are permitted some temperament simply because we are women!

Granted we are not, as a sex, the strong silent type. There would be less reason for men if we were. But just as men have no right to excuse their domestic or spiritual inactivity solely on their heritage of strength and silence, neither do women have a right to excuse their irritability and nagging and unbridled tongues on the fact that, by nature, women are just like that.

Dispositions are not inward things. They are outward. To try to control your disposition by what you know to be right intellectually or morally is a waste of time. It is somewhat admirable, but quite futile. At least it won't work under all circumstances and with all heritages.

A woman's disposition is merely an outward sign of what she really *is* within. An outward sign of what is predominant within her inner self.

If she is predominant there, her disposition shows it.

If Christ is predominant there, her disposition shows that, too.

Then what are we to do? If we know Christ lives within us, and we are still displaying ourselves via our dispositions, what are we to do? Two things: First, we are to remember that He works with our minds according to the way He created them. And He created them able to form habits. If we remember this, we will realize that we must form the habit of *choosing* to let Christ act through us. To form new habits takes time, and if we remember this, we will not fall into the senseless pit of discouragement when we do not break the old habits and form shining new ones overnight! And then, after realizing that under all circumstances we must *choose* whether we are to be ourselves or let Him be Himself, we must actually make the choice and act on it.

Christ is within us to control our total personalities. But He is above all interested in building our characters and so He never overpowers us by His might. In His love, He waits for us to choose! Each time we choose to let Him be Himself through us, we are being added to at the center of our beings. Being added to by something of the very nature of Christ Himself.

Jesus Christ would not do us the injustice of waving a celestial magic wand over our dispositions. This would be easier for us now, but harder in the final analysis. He is interested in remaking our characters so that we will be at home and familiar with our surroundings and friends throughout all eternity.

We can begin right now by thanking Him for our disposition defects! After all, if we don't see them, we'll never come to Him for healing. The defects themselves are only outward symptoms that the wrong person is at the controls within the depths of our personalities.

3

The Difference Christ Makes ...
IN YOUR CONSCIOUS MIND

3

The Difference Christ Makes...

IN YOUR CONSCIOUS MIND

It is unfortunate that this chapter and the next cannot be written and read at exactly the same time. But since we are still living *in* time we can only approach ideas consecutively.

Psychology has loosely divided our minds into *conscious* and *subconscious*. This is relatively accurate. In this chapter and the next we are going to take an honest, non-technical, and I hope, practical look at both.

To all appearances, the conscious and subconscious are separate. It must always be remembered, however, that they make up the *whole* of the mind. We control our conscious minds and we do not have direct control over the actual functioning of our subconscious mind. But they are inseparably related. They hold terrifying influence one over the other.

Your conscious mind is the part of your mind with which you knowingly think. It is the part of your mind with which you form habits. It is the part of your mind with which you make decisions. It is the part of your mind with which you reason. With which you form likes and dislikes. With which you make judgments.

It is the part of your mind over which you have control.

You have definite *influence* over your subconscious mind, as we shall see in the next chapter, but over your conscious mind you have *control.* We do not always make use of this gift from God, this ability to control our thoughts, but we do have it. And with this conscious mind we decide what kind of conscious mind it will be!

The Bible says, "God looketh on the heart." He does. But when the Bible speaks of the heart, I believe it includes the mind and the will, as well as the seat of our emotions. So, I believe that with our conscious minds we control the very attitudes of our hearts.

Most of the problems about which I learn, from personal conversation with women or from their letters, have to do with these key words: peace, poise, energy, worry, anxiety or fear.

Women seem to be uneasy, nervous, weary, worried, anxious or afraid. All of these conditions are interrelated. What is said here about one will apply equally to all.

But let's look at these words one by one, and see how we can change them to their opposites through a *conscious* action on our part. Before we look at each word, however, we must look at the fact of Christ. When we receive Him as our Saviour, He comes to live in our mortal bodies. This means He also makes His home in our *conscious minds.* And since they are under our control, we and we alone decide whether we are going to attempt to handle them in a somewhat Christian manner ourselves, or whether we are going to make the decision to turn the control of our conscious minds over to Christ. This can be done at one moment of decision. But its results are gradual. (It is here that the conscious mind is in a different relationship to Christ from that of the subconscious mind.) Where our conscious minds are concerned, He *requires* our cooperation.

Jesus always leaves the final choice to us.

He did not say, "I will drag you along with me." He said, "Follow me." We decide, and *then* His Spirit empowers us to act on our decisions, provided we have decided in His favor. (Let it be remembered that no one needs to be empowered to act selfishly. We were born with that power!)

Paul did not say, "When you become a follower of Jesus Christ you will never think on anything but lovely things." He said, "*Let* this mind be in you . . . *think* on these things."

Since the New Testament is the greatest textbook on depth psychology ever written, it should surprise no one to find in it these truths concerning our minds. And since the New Testament was written by the One who thought up the human mind in the first place, it should surprise no one that He knows and works with this mind exactly as He created it.

And one of the strong characteristics of the conscious mind is its ability to *form habits*. Habits do not form overnight. They are not broken overnight. God knows this. He, for reasons of His own, created the conscious mind this way.

Keeping this firmly in mind, let's look at the chronic ailments seemingly native to the conscious mind of modern woman.

Lack of peace. Is this characteristic of the modern *Christian* woman? Yes, it is. I have placed it first, because letter by letter, it comes up again and again more frequently than any other in my mail from women. My heart aches over these letters.

My heart aches for the women and it also aches for Christ! They are, for the most part, devout, sincere believers. And they almost always ask, "What is wrong with me? I know it can't be the Lord. It must be my fault."

Yes. But I have come to see that these women are depend-

ing upon prayer, the Bible, meetings, their experience, my experience, Christian books—almost everything but Christ Himself! They have not allowed the great simplicity of who He *is*
dawn on their conscious minds. Right to the point goes Paul
on this subject: "He *is* our peace." And he has promised
never to leave us nor forsake us. "Lo, I am with you alway."
Peace is not something we can wrap in a package or store
away on a shelf. It is not a "something" at all. It is a Person.
Peace is Jesus Christ Himself. He has given us a conscious
mind with which to take hold of this. We control that conscious mind. Whether you feel peaceful or not as you read
these lines, if you belong to Jesus Christ, you *have peace*
because you have Him.

One of the greatest tricks of the strange depths of our human personalities is to cause us to think that just because we
don't feel a certain way, we are not that way. Just by making
use of my God-given conscious mind, I have decided to cultivate the habit of remembering that He will never leave
me. I may leave Him, but He will never leave me. And "He
is our peace." Therefore, I can know and have peace, Himself, in the midst of great weeping. In the midst of nerve-
shattering confusion. In the midst of misunderstanding and
anger. And *as* I use my conscious mind to remember this, I
find, when I least expect it, that some sense of this peace
returns to my emotions, too.

The next most often complained about state of mind is *lack
of poise.* Letters come which say, "I *tried* to keep calm. I tried
to control myself, but when he let me have it as he did last
Saturday night, etc., etc." Or "How can I overcome this terrible shyness? I just can't pray aloud. I was asked to lead
devotions in the new church I have just joined and I actually
lied to get out of it! I said I was ill and stayed at home—and
wept and wept for shame."

You may think these two illustrations are contradictory.

No, they're basically alike. One woman couldn't control her temper and the other couldn't control her shyness. One seems "worse" than the other. But both instances show definite lack of *poise*. No one is going to be perfectly poised all the time and under all circumstances. You must accept yourself as you are. You are not someone else. You are you. But here again, *discipline* of the conscious mind which God has given you is the answer. Do I mean force yourself to be quiet or force yourself to speak aloud? No. *Cultivate the habit* of remembering who it is who has come to live within you. And rely on His Poise! The quiet that comes from the knowledge that He is there will in time restore your poise.

This does not come overnight. Developing a habit is a slow —sometimes discouragingly slow—process. But because of the way in which God created your conscious mind, it is never a hopeless process. You can depend entirely upon Him. But you had better act as though in one way, at least, you are depending entirely upon yourself. What is that way? In the matter of *continuing* even after you have fallen down, in the matter of the cultivation of the habit of remembering that *Christ lives within you.*

Somehow He always manages to make things work out for our character-building. If He waved a magic wand over your head and shut your mouth when you wanted to "sound off" or if He spoke a magic word over you and whisked your shyness into a Celestial Ashcan, what would it profit you? What would it profit me? Soon we would fancy ourselves privileged daughters of the Most High. We would become so smug and self-righteous, we'd lose our last earthly friend because · e would have become unbearable company! God wants to .ake us "good company." He wants to naturalize us by a supernatural process known as the working of His Spirit within us.

But we must be willing to cooperate with our conscious

minds and form the habit of remembering that we are embarked on an eternal adventure with God Himself.

What of your *energy*? Again and again I hear, "I'm just so
tired all the time, I can't have an adequate prayer time. I
can't attend church regularly, etc." Some of us are tired
physically and for admirable reasons. I personally don't think
I'd be able to get through one week as a mother and homemaker! I'd collapse in a heap by the ironing board or become
a willing candidate for the nearest mental institution.

A lady in Iowa said to me recently, "If I had to travel the
way you travel and still write a whole book a year, I wouldn't
last a month!"

She had four small children, a husband, a family laundry
every day, a six-room house, a Sunday school class, was the
family chauffeur, sang in the choir and was president of the
P.T.A. She probably would last longer than a month in my
life, but I still set my limit to a week if I were in hers.

God knows all of this. He knows this lady in Iowa loves
children. So do I, as long as they belong (at quite a distance)
to someone else. My nerves would be naked and screaming
in no time with four small children around me. This woman
would be, as she put it "pulling her hair and shrieking" if she
had to sit at a typewriter just one day. She likes to read, but
she wants someone else to work over the writing. I feel the
same way about her children. I enjoy them as long as someone else has to take care of them.

In her position, I'd be excessively weary most of the time.
In mine, she would be. And yet, while God puts us, if He
has His way in our lives, where He knows we will function
best, fortune and circumstances and bad judgments sometimes put us into circumstances where we are not suited to
the job.

Where is the God factor here?

Once more, it is the conscious mind which must be put

into play. He has promised that if we will come to Him, He will *give* us rest, no matter where we are.

Circumstances may be forcing you to stay in a job you hate. You may feel your talents are worth a great deal more. Perhaps they are. Perhaps they're not. But one thing I know, if Christ dwells in you, then the "ground on which you stand is holy ground." Because He is standing on it, too. And because He is a redeemer God, He will give you a way to make creative use of even your unpleasant surroundings. If you have read my life story *The Burden Is Light*, you know He did it for me. He acts according to what He knows is the right timing. He does not act according to what we keep telling Him about time in our prayers.

He has promised that He will give us rest no matter where we are. And He is a God of His Word.

What does this mean when my physical energy is all gone at the end of a long day of travel, speaking, writing letters and (most tiring of all) constantly giving out to people? What does it mean after your long day of whatever it is that fills your days? If you and I have learned the habit of remembering that "He is our peace," much of our physical weariness is absorbed in that knowing.

Not all of it. There is nothing in the New Testament which tells us that we are not going to get tired. Jesus did. But the extra weariness that settles upon the heart and body of those who are irritable, jumpy, maladjusted or uneasy, is lifted by remembering that peace is a Person. As I have already told you, during the first day's writing on this book (all of which I threw away!) I was tired all day. When I readjusted my thinking (making use of the conscious mind which I control) and began to remember whose I am, the weariness left me. On the second day of writing, I accomplished twice as much, went out to dinner at night, attended a board meeting, and still felt like studying the book criticisms in the

Saturday Review when I got home at eleven in the evening!

Much weariness comes from disturbance within us. But if we remember that He is also within us, rest comes. Not from a trick of self-hypnosis or auto-suggestion, but from the simple use of our conscious minds in forming the habit of remembering that He is always here.

Many people recite the twenty-third Psalm in order to go to sleep at night. It is not the words themselves that give you rest. It is the presence of the Shepherd Himself in your life. Think on Him.

Worry and *anxiety* and *fear* are playmates. They play havoc with our poor conscious minds. We fall victims of them. All three of them. One woman said to me, "What will keep my family together if I don't worry?"

Poor, poor woman. Perhaps the conditions in her family were cause for worry from a human standpoint. But the conditions at Calvary and the present conditions in heaven are the antidote! In my very first book *Discoveries,* when I had been a Christian only three years, I wrote about *worry.* I used a definition about which hundreds of people have written me in the years since the little book was published. I did not know who wrote the definition then and even with all those letters, I still have not discovered who wrote it. But acknowledging someone's great insight, I'd like to repeat it here. "*Worry* is a cycle of inefficient thought, whirling about a center of *fear.*"

Yes, *worry* and *anxiety* and *fear* are playmates. Whirling playmates. Demonic little authors of confusion. Where there is worry, there is fear. Where there is anxiety, there is also fear. Worry and anxiety *do* whirl about a center of fear.

But is the Bible wrong when we are told that "Perfect love casts out fear"? And are you replying, "I know the Bible is right, but I still have my fear"?

Let's examine this more closely. Is fear in the center of

your life? Are you seemingly helpless to do anything about it? Good. Because while you can't do anything about your fear, you *can* once more make use of your conscious mind to *allow* Jesus Christ to step into the center of your life and He will cast the fear out!

Does the Bible mean Jesus Christ when it says that "perfect love casts out fear"? Yes, it does. "God is love." Is Jesus Christ one and the same with God? Yes, He is, or He Himself was mistaken, because remember (recall right now with your *conscious mind*) that Jesus said, "I and the Father are one . . . if you have seen me, you have seen the Father."

It is difficult, impossible at certain times of great fear, for us to lay hold of what seems to be only a spiritual principle about a spiritual phenomenon called love. However, when we use the minds God gave us to think through to the fact that this love is not a spiritual phenomenon but a Person, miracles occur! A Person *can* literally "cast out." A principle can't, but a Person can. And most glorious of all, we can know this Person. We can know what He is like. We can see His heart exposed on a cross. We can experience His healing touch on our minds.

We must not be impatient when our conscious minds are not changed as rapidly as we think they should be. After all, if we have given the control of those minds over to Jesus Christ, we can trust His timing in reforming our thought patterns. He made those conscious minds in the first place. Surely if we use them to form the habit of remembering what He is really like, we can leave the results to Him, can't we?

Here it is well to remember that anything we do thirty-five times becomes a habit!

In the next chapter, we will look at our subconscious minds. In them we find the hidden factory in which most of our fears are manufactured.

The Difference Christ Makes . . .

IN YOUR SUBCONSCIOUS

MIND

4

The Difference Christ Makes . . .

IN YOUR SUBCONSCIOUS MIND

Your *conscious* and *subconscious* make up the whole of your mind. One cannot be intelligently considered without the other.

One directly influences the other.

It is really a closed circuit.

Fears and worry and self-consciousness and unrest plague the conscious mind, but they are stored in the subconscious!

It has been helpful to me to realize that our subconscious minds are like baskets. Into them is dropped *everything* that passes through our conscious minds!

This is a terrifying thought.

But it is true. Everything we say, hear, think or act upon "drops," as it were, into the basket of the subconscious. What a ghastly state of confusion and distortion and ugliness and sin must prevail in our subconscious minds! But we might as well face it. We *can* control our conscious minds, and by discipline and association and memory, bring some manner of order to them. But except as we control what drops *into*

our subconscious minds, we have no active means of controlling them.

And to add to this seemingly tragic state of things, we are
said to be nine-tenths subconscious. Like an iceberg, we are
mostly "under water." When we turn to Jesus Christ and determine with our conscious minds to follow Him, only one
tenth of us has turned!

We perceive something of His truth and His way of life
and our conscious minds fall under His influence. The degree
to which they show this influence depends upon our sincerity
and willingness, but it also depends upon the *length of time*
our conscious thought patterns have been formed.

If a man has been running to a bottle for escape and sur-
cease from his problems for twenty years, he will seldom
break this pattern at once. It is well known to anyone who
works with alcoholics that some become intoxicated as many
as half a dozen times after their conversions to Christ, before
the patterns of the years are finally broken.

It is one of the great tragedies of Christendom for us to
judge the authenticity of a conversion experience by the
length of time required to replace the old patterns by new
ones. This is superficial thinking and shows a complete lack
of knowledge of how the conscious mind works.

Granted, then, that however long it may take, the conscious
mind does in some degree begin to show a change from the
old way to the new, upon conversion to Jesus Christ, what
happens in the subconscious?

We have said that it is like a basket. When God takes over
the human mind at conversion, He takes over the subconscious with all its frightening contents. He would be less than
God if He did not.

I can only thank Him for being the kind of God He is, when
I remember the chaos of my own subconscious mind when
I became a Christian. Actually, I hadn't given my subcon-

scious a thought in the beginning. I was too excited with the new, shining concepts which were crowding into my conscious mind.

But as the weeks passed by, I began to be haunted during the day by the dreams I experienced at night. My conscious mind was made up. I wanted to follow Jesus Christ. I wanted to belong to Him. I wanted Him to belong to me.

But my subconscious mind evidently hadn't heard the news of my conversion!

I would dream at night of my old life, of the friends I had loved so much, of the best of the high points of a life which had been spent in the pursuit of success and pleasure. I would awaken, restless and disturbed. On those days I didn't want to read the Bible or pray. And the temptation to run back to the dear, old familiar ways began to take hold of my conscious mind. The dreams came from my subconscious. But my conscious mind paid the price. They *are* both a part of the whole.

As with almost every new Christian, now and then I would question whether "anything had really happened to me" at all! But fortunately I was not persuaded to become a Christian because of a process called salvation or a promise of a thrilling experience. I was persuaded to become a Christian because Jesus Christ, Himself, was held up to me. And so I went straight to Him with the problem of my dreams.

One of the first things I was told about Him was that He loved me so much nothing was unimportant to Him where I was concerned. I believed this, simply, as a child believes things he is told and so I went to Him about my dreams. And I said something like this to Him: "Lord, I know that my subconscious mind is nine-tenths of me. And now that I believe You created me, You must have created my subconscious, too. And if You did, then You know I don't have any control over it. I know I have dropped many, many wrong things down into it through the years when I didn't know You even existed. But there's nothing I can do about that now. What can You do? I know You can do something about changing the very depths of my subconscious mind. And so, beginning tonight, I am going to make a *conscious* act of handing my *subconscious* over to You the very last thing before I go to sleep. And I'll do it every night. Will You please untangle it for me?"

I did my part, and, of course, so did He.

Almost at once my dreams began to show conflict! I might still dream the same things, but somewhere in the dream would be a new ingredient. A conflict of some kind *because* of Jesus Christ. Before I made that simple transaction with Him, the dreams had run the gamut of the old life, and I was in them as I had been *before* my conversion.

No longer. From that time to this day, when and if I happen to dream of my old life in any way, I awaken with a smile. Sometimes I even laugh with relief at His determined invasion of my subconscious mind.

A psychiatrist can dig things out of our subconscious minds and often just the seeing will release us wonderfully. But the best any competent psychiatrist can do is show us our trouble and advise us how to learn to live with it. I am thankful for all the men and women who offer this helpful service to humanity. As Christians we should urge Christian young people to enter the field. But most of us don't need a psychiatrist. And followers of Jesus Christ belong to the Great Psychiatrist. The One who created the human mind in the beginning.

Allow this to enter your thought life once and for all: The Holy Spirit of God *can*—and *wants* to—change your subconscious mind. Perhaps this is the part of us in which His work is most effective! If you have received Christ as your Saviour, the Holy Spirit is already at work in your subconscious as well as your conscious mind. But it would appear that we greatly facilitate His work in the depths of our personalities when, with our conscious minds, we make a love offering to Him of all that we cannot control in ourselves.

If your conscious thoughts are knotted and held by the fear of not being loved, of being a nobody, of expressing yourself, or if you seem to be held by even a nameless fear, a good psychiatrist could no doubt help you.

And possibly your fear of not being loved, your basic fear-choked sense of insecurity can be traced to some unfortunate condition of your childhood or to some hard blow life has dealt you. Realizing this is a step in the right direction. But time after time, I have watched the Holy Spirit of God set free a fear-clogged mind simply by some *direct contact* with Jesus Christ Himself.

If Christians are to go through their earthly lives still bound by fear and worry and anxiety patterns, then Jesus must have been wrong when He said, "I am come that they might have life, and that they might have it more abundantly."

Either He meant that or He did not.

With many women who have spoken to me about their fears and worries, you may be reminding me in your thoughts that you have already received Jesus Christ as your Saviour. But still you are afraid.

This was the situation with someone whom I will call Marian. I met her during a speaking engagement in a large eastern city. And of all the fearful and disturbed women with whom I have spoken, Marian was the most fearful. She was extremely intelligent. Her humor and her insight into things spiritual and secular interested me. But by her own admission she had poured out her problem to "dozens of leaders" of all faiths. For some reason psychiatry had not helped her either. Her physical condition showed the marks of her emotional battles. She was ill physically and emotionally. And she was being slowly frightened to death by life!

The weeks passed and no help came to her. Then one night we met again in another city where I was speaking. Frankly, I was looking forward to her company but not to a discussion of her problems. I had heard it all by letter, over and over and over and over. She appeared to be locked permanently in a prison of fear. She seemed to want out, but nothing I said, nothing anyone else said, had helped. She had become a Christian several years before. But there she was sitting across the table from me in the hotel dining room that night still trembling and talking in wretched, painful circles.

I asked to be excused for a half hour and went to my own room. I had prayed for her until I didn't know anything else to say to the Lord about her. And yet, there she was waiting for me to come to her room and help her! I went to Him again. "Lord, You've brought this evening about. You died for Marian and You died for me. I'm all out of things to say to her. I'm not a professional counselor. I'm tired, and I'm desperate, and so is she. Take over!"

In her room a few minutes later, we began to talk. Immediately, her *old patterns* took over. "I want to be free. I do! I've tried. It just doesn't work with me. I know you're going to tell me that what has been working for Christians for almost two thousand years will work for me, too. You've already told me that you couldn't follow a God who would withhold His power from even one person! I know I can't be a special case. But here I am! Nothing helps."

I started to try to tell her again about the fact of His presence. Suddenly I was stopped in the telling. And I found myself no longer talking to Marian at all. I was talking to Christ Himself.

She had a block against what she called "regular prayer." Someone had tried to *teach* her to pray properly once and had snapped her fingers at Marian when she didn't "pray properly." Remembering her panic over this unfortunate event, I just sat there in the chair with my eyes open and spoke directly to Christ.

"You're here, Lord. You said you would be when two or more are gathered together in Your Name. Marian and I are here in Your Name and we're stuck! Now, without any more formality, I'm going to ask You to do what we can't do. Will you, right now, begin to melt down this strange resistance in Marian to Your love? Will You do it right now, Lord? This minute! Will you give her power to speak to You, too? Now."

I looked at Marian. She was writhing and so tense I feared for her physical well-being. But I had just thrown the whole issue over onto Him and I determined to wait to see what He would do with this fear-bound child of His.

In the same voice which I had used when I spoke to Him (an ordinary conversational voice) I said: "Marian, tell Him you love Him." She just looked at me and my heart squeezed a little because I remembered the well-meaning friend who had snapped her fingers at her, trying to "teach her to pray."

I might have wanted to do that once. But no longer. During the past two years I, too, had been melted down by the almost unbelievable love of Christ Himself. I had dropped "techniques." And so, I could just sit there quietly and speak first to Him and then to her.

"Lord, here she is. Will you break down this wall of resistance in her? You know what caused it in the first place. You know what she needs right now. We don't, but You do."

Then to Marian I said, "Try just one word. Turn your whole being toward all you know of Christ and say His Name. Just say 'Jesus.' "

The muscles in her face tightened. And then after a long minute a little tense, frightened voice said, "Jesus."

I continued talking to Him quietly. Very, very quietly. I

longed to avoid any tone of voice or phrasing which might make Him seem remote to her. I knew He would cast out her fear if He had an opening. Aloud, so she could hear me, I asked Him to keep me sensitive to her as she was, at that minute there in that hotel room.

And then we sat together during a long, long silence.

My tendency has always been to talk too much, to try to communicate what I have discovered. His Love has overcome that tendency I now know, because I waited out the long, anxious, moments with her in silence.

A long, long time passed and then she spoke to Him.

"Jesus . . . I ask You to break it down in me. Whatever it is."

More silence.

Then it occurred to me to ask her one simple question. "Marian, would you like to tell Him you love Him?"

Her reply was an old familiar volley at me. The fear-pattern took over again. "But, do I love Him? I've tried, Genie. Honestly, I've tried, but I'm scared. I'm just plain scared, I—." She stopped the nervous chatter. Her voice changed suddenly from the rapid, hoarse frightened rat-tat-tat of almost meaningless words to a slow, hesitant, but suddenly quite childlike whisper.

I shall never, never forget what she said to Him then.

"Jesus? Jesus, are You listening? Well, if You are, I—I just want—." For a moment, I thought she might faint. But thank God, I kept quiet.

The same childlike whisper, slowly, very, very fearfully. "Jesus? I—I just want to tell—You—I, *do* love You."

And then we did nothing for another long time except sit there with Him.

With you, in your own particular fear-trauma, there may be other words, other circumstances. But *anyone*, with a normal conscious mind, no matter how torn it is with fear and dread and anxiety, can make a direct contact with the Person of Jesus Christ. Anyone. Anyone. Marian's *conscious* act of speaking to Him personally (not to me, to Him!) made the pinpoint opening which set His Spirit free to begin His miracle of healing in her *subconscious* mind.

For years, her subconscious had been cluttered with the fears and dreads and anxieties which tortured and twisted her conscious mind. That night in that strange hotel room by His grace, through a direct answer to our request, she had ventured one simple act of contacting *Him*. She spoke to Him. She responded to Him. She told Him she loved Him!

I doubt if she felt much love for Him as she spoke the words. But she spoke them. And the seemingly high locked gates to the recesses of her very being flew open!

Her life is still full of trials and unsolved problems. Her physical condition is anything but good. But her letters now are a benediction to me as I write this book. She is talking much and freely to Jesus Himself now. And she is asking Him every day that He will be able to get through these words of mine to your heart, particularly if it is tormented with fear as hers was.

As I see it, we make the opening through our *conscious* minds for Him to invade our tangled *subconscious* minds with the love that always, always heals whatever it touches.

This dependable principle works whether your problem is fear, worry, pride, selfishness or self-deception.

We must keep firmly in our *conscious minds* that neither our conscious nor our subconscious is a mystery to Christ. He knows. He created them both. "Without Him was not anything made that was made."

5

The Difference Christ Makes . . .

IN YOUR REFUTATION

5

The Difference Christ Makes . . .

IN YOUR REPUTATION

Perhaps the average Christian woman does not give much thought to her reputation.

This is a major tragedy.

But I think I understand why it is that so little emphasis is placed upon such an important part of a woman's life. Most Christian women have lived such sheltered lives, and are still living such sheltered lives, that unless an emergency situation arises, they feel no need to think about it.

This is the outward reason.

There is, however, an inner reason and this constitutes the tragedy. We have a superficial, false definition of reputation. I hope in these pages to get down to essentials.

And because we will be handling essentials, there will be no comment at all upon obvious externals such as smoking, social drinking, being seen in the so-called "wrong" places, breaking shop windows or beating your husband in public.

We are attempting to be honest as we ask what difference it makes whether or not a woman's personality is controlled by Jesus Christ.

He is concerned with your *heart*.

With the attitudes which govern the central core of your being. With the hidden depths of your personality. What is inside will come out sooner or later. Lopping off a few showy externals is as far removed from the real meaning of Christianity as it is possible to go.

There are many areas which need exploring here. We shall look at only three. But their general direction, which is *inward*, should give us a key to further self-examination beyond the content of this chapter.

What do people say about you when you're not around? Wouldn't we all like to know! But a few minutes of honesty on our part right now will give us a good, general idea. We may not like what we see, but until we see our need, God can do nothing toward filling that need.

What words do people use in describing or discussing you? Do they call you *lovely?* If so, good. God can make great use of lovely looking women.

Do they call you *lovable?* Also good. The more contagious your natural personality, the simpler it is for you to enter other hearts.

But the first key to unlocking the secret of the impression you really make on other people is neither of those words, although in some sense both will follow this one. Ask yourself right now, if so far as you know, according to your own knowledge of yourself based upon your acts and deeds *and* the type of persons whom you attract, do people call you *loving?*

What have you done this week, this month? Have you taken good care of your family, or your job, and have you dispatched your church or social responsibilities and have you donated according to your income tax deductions to some charitable cause?

If so, well and good. But don't most people do this? Most

people in your social strata? Where, outside of your family and church circles, have you honestly *given of yourself* when you didn't really have to do it?

Where, specifically, have you been *loving?*

Where have you made some small or large gesture toward someone who might be too selfish to say thank you? Have you given some of your money to anyone who doesn't represent a foundation or other deductible organization? Have you taken time to send a card or write a letter to someone for *no other reason* than that he or she needs that card or letter?

No one knows better than I that "by grace are ye saved." This is not an examination to determine your salvation. This is an examination to try to find some *result* of it!

To whom have you shown love without their even knowing about it? Literally and figuratively, have you always taken off the price tags before you gave?

Or, does your love seem to thrive best on response? If you've sacrificed yourself, was there no demand in you whatever for thanks?

Recently I was riding on a train through the Middle West. In the seat behind me, an obviously moral soul held forth without ceasing, for her poor husband's and every other ear in our section of the parlor car in which we were riding. I had taken a parlor car in order to avoid conversation as I began outlining this book. *I* avoided it myself, but I quickly gave up the outline and settled back to be at times uproariously entertained, and at others brought upright in my seat with amazement, as this good sister clicked off the miles with her tongue.

"Bill, we're goin' home to bury poor old Mort. And we're gonna' do the right things. All of 'em. Not just some. All. We've all got to go sooner or later. Mort's gone. God rest his soul. And it's up to you and me to do the right things. And one person I'm gonna' do right by is his widow. Maud's a lovely

person. A *lovely* person. Wears the prettiest hats. Good lookin'
woman. And just as good as she looks, too. Yes, sir, Maud's
just the way she looks. Good. But now, you take her sister,
Madge. I wouldn't stir from the front porch swing if that
woman needed help right in our front yard! Why, when her
mother passed on, I went out of my way to be kind to her. I
baked cookies and took some of my pickles and some of my
best jelly over. I stayed up part of the night so's she wouldn't
be by herself that first night. I even went all the way to the
cemetery when I had such a bad cold I thought I'd be the
next one. But do you think Madge ever even wrote me one
little note of thanks? She did not! Not one scratch, Bill. Not
one. I believe in followin' the Good Book, you know that, but
Madge *never* did for others. Others like me did for Madge.
Madge never did for others, Bill. But, with Maud—that's a
different horse of another color. Oh, I'll do for Maud when we
get there. And you can just bet your bottom dollar Maud'll
thank me for it, too. Yes, sir, she will."

This was a well-meaning Christian woman. At least she reminded poor, patient Bill of her Christianity for all to hear
over and over during the six hours in which she kept tempo
with the speed of the streamlined train. I'm sure she did many
kind things for people. In fact, she convinced me that she
did! But always she held the mirror (clean and polished as I'm
sure all her mirrors are) for everyone to see the limited extent
of no more than average human love.

She "did for others" according to the *response* she received
from them.

We may not publicize our activities in quite such concen-
trated doses as this woman publicized hers. But our lives and
our actions do. And let me make it clear that human love,
even at its best *does* thrive on response!

One mother admitted to me that she finds it much easier to
love her eight-year-old boy when he is obeying her. It doesn't

mean she stops loving him when he doesn't. But hers is a human love. And human love does thrive on response from its object.

Here, then is one blind spot in the insight of many Christian women. We fail to realize that most of the time our love is merely *human love.* We justify ourselves by the nice things we do for the Mauds in our lives who thank us. We skip the Madges who forget to write notes of gratitude for our magnificence. We fail to see that human love is just not enough to cover the frailties of human nature. It is here that one of the most pointed differences between a self-controlled personality and a Christ-controlled personality springs up to confront us!

God's love seems to thrive on suffering, *not* on response. His heart is gladdened by our response, but I can tell you that I am many times more aware of His love when I am disobedient toward Him than when I am sitting in my "chair of heavenly bliss" reading Scriptures about it! It is with this everlasting, steady love which knows no mood changes, that God melts me into repentance. I need a more thankful heart. I fail to thank Him most of the time. But my ungratefulness does not change His love. It only demonstrates it!

And certainly none of us has human love to equal His. Ours isn't even the same kind of love as God's love. It is not a difference in *degree.* His isn't an improved human love. It is a totally different *kind* of love.

But we have access to His love. Not only to receive it but to make use of it. Christ lives within us and when He comes He brings His love with Him.

Christian women are few and far between who have the reputation of being *loving.* This sad state of affairs is true, I believe, in part at least because we do not remember that we have all the love that poured from the Cross of Calvary at our disposal. Few of us are attracted to unlovely, ungrateful people. But they need love more than the grateful ones. The love which can pour from a Christ-controlled personality *can* love the unlovely, *can* love the ungrateful.

A woman whose personality is Christ-controlled can be known as *loving*. I remember one such woman well. Her name was Carrie. I doubt if I even learned her last name. But she came to the prayer room after I had spoken, leading a large, overly made-up, unkempt, half-intoxicated younger woman by the hand. Carrie was a little woman about seventy. For twelve years she had been head and hand and heart holding this alcoholic woman whom no one else would even invite to her home. The people of the church talked about it. They admired Carrie and thought her some special kind of saint. And at last the night had come. This woman had broken dishes and sworn and fallen down in her drunkenness all over Carrie's little cottage for twelve years. This night she walked like a penitent child to a prayer room beside the woman who had shown her Christ's love.

I relaxed about that woman when I left town after the engagement was over. I knew she would be able to grow up in her new life in Christ, because she would be bathed in His love through Carrie, for as long as it took to break her old patterns.

It was nothing I said that brought the woman to the end of herself. She had been gradually melted through the years by love, Himself, through a simple, plain Christian woman who was willing to take the inconvenience and the heartache involved for her, as He poured His love *through* her to the rebellious woman who needed it so much.

In her community in the little Illinois town, Carrie has the reputation of a *loving* Christian woman. She doesn't preach. She doesn't try to prove her point. She doesn't argue. She loves. She can. She is Christ-controlled. And He is love.

Do you have the reputation of being *loving?*

Do you have the reputation of being *sensitive* to other people? I didn't say sensitive *toward* them, I said sensitive *to* them. Can you *identify* with other persons? Or do you sit in judgment upon them?

To me, the key to Christianity is that God *identified* with us on every point. "He was in all points tempted like as we are." And right now, I hope you will check yourself closely on this point of *identification*. Are you able to project your own personality into the personality of someone whom you dislike? Are you willing to do it? Are you willing to project your personality into the personality of someone whom you don't consider your equal? (If there is someone whom you *don't* consider your equal, you had better make a double check!)

What is your reputation here? Do all types of people feel free to pour out their hearts to you? Are you considered a bustling, busy, hard-working church woman who writes checks and passes mite boxes avidly for foreign missions? But would you welcome a Negro to your home for dinner? And are you shocked at certain sins which you haven't, by grace, committed yourself? If you would refuse anyone the right to your home or if you are easily shocked, then you are not *identifying*. You are not calling on the Holy Spirit of the Christ (who died with His arms stretched out toward the whole world) to enable you to place yourself in the other person's position. If someone doesn't live up to your standards, would *you* be living up to his if you had had his background?

Perhaps you are a Bible teacher. Or at least you love to read your Bible and rather pride yourself on knowing your way around in it. All this is good. But does the very fact that you are *sure* you have the truth shut you out from someone who doesn't yet see that the Bible is the written-down Word of God? If someone disagrees with your doctrine, are your arms open and your heart exposed as His were that dark afternoon on Calvary?

There is at least one more way in which we should check ourselves where reputation is concerned. That is our reputation for being able to *face reality*. Are you *realistic?* Or do you embroider things to make them palatable to you? God is the great Realist. He is Reality. He sees us exactly as we are. "While we were yet sinners, Christ died for us."

It is hard, for example, for some mothers to admit that their daughters need a Saviour. Mothers are lovely people, but they have a self-protecting way of making their own idealized images of their children. "*My* child would never do a thing like that."

Any child may do anything!

"All have sinned and come short of the glory of God."

When we refuse to face reality, we refuse to face life. Any beginning of a refusal to face people and circumstances as they are is the beginning of genuine neurosis, says Dr. Karen Horney. I believe this, because one refusal piles upon another and soon we are living in our own idealized false worlds behind a barricade of neurotic notions.

A mother, for example, who refuses to face the fact that her son or daughter could commit a so-called flagrant sin, is establishing a poor reputation with this child she loves, in all three areas which we have discussed. She is not being *loving* in the truest sense, she is not *identifying* with the child, and she is not being *realistic*. She is telling herself that this just couldn't happen to her daughter or to her son. And with this child, she is establishing the reputation of someone difficult to talk to, impossible to confide in.

God became a human being for our sake. We, too, must be human beings for the sake of those whose lives we touch. And being human is not a bad thing. It is what we are! It is being realistic. It is being natural. It is keeping our feet on the ground of human understanding. It is staying off the pedestal of our own idealized images of ourselves.

I want the reputation of being a human being who sees all the potential good and evil in herself, but who also sees the potential of her personality linked with the personality of Christ. This kind of Christian woman is easy socially, mentally, emotionally and spiritually. Easy to know. Easy to talk to. Easy to love. Because she loves.

Christ lives within us, and when we choose to do so, we *can* bear to look at things as they are, simply because He is already seeing them that way. We can *identify* with His sensitivity, we can *love* with His love, we can be *realistic* because He is Reality.

A woman's reputation as a Christian is *not*, if we are being realistic, based on what she does and does not do. Her real reputation is built and colored according to who is in control *in the depths* of her personality.

6

The Difference Christ Makes . . .

IN YOUR WORK

6

The Difference Christ Makes . . .

IN YOUR WORK

"Woman's work is never done." Neither is modern woman's work ever classified! She is free now to do almost any kind of work which interests her. Had I lived in the days before women were set free, I should have headed all parades with the largest banner of all held high proclaiming our rights to be *people.*

Men have always been permitted to be people.

We have just recently made it.

But thank God, we have made it. And now and forever, as long as the earth shall last, I hope that it will never be possible to classify woman's work. In this chapter we will be speaking of women who may be homemakers, office workers, teachers, doctors, lecturers, nurses, chemists, manufacturers, advertising executives, electronic experts, saleswomen, writers, ad infinitum. But they all have womanhood and work in common.

We will use actual illustrations from the lives of a few who have proven to themselves and to those with whom they work, that there is an amazing difference even in these daily tasks when a woman's personality is controlled by Jesus Christ.

First of all, in one sense, all women are homemakers. This is our natural instinct. I have been in my own home approximately only three months out of each of the past three or four years. But I still care about it. I am still interested in its decor. There was left out of my make-up entirely the usual womanly ingredient of loving to cook and sew and bake and mend. I can broil steaks and make a fair garlic salad, but I still can't sew on a button so that it will stay sewed on or make a bed properly. Personally, I should hate the confinement of regular housework. I would make a dreadful full-time homemaker and wife and mother. I wouldn't like the roles and I would not be successful at any of the three.

But still I dare to write to you who are homemakers and wives and mothers, because I am a woman, too, and because in my own life I have experienced and am experiencing the vast difference between my work with and without Jesus Christ at the controls. You see I have lived most of my life with myself at the controls. The difference is one to inspire great lyrics.

I hope many of you who are reading this are still students in high school or college. You are women, too. And I am convinced that no work you will ever have to do will be harder than what you are doing now. I spent almost half of the years of my life in schools and universities. Life never exacts more of us than it does during those years. So, without a doubt, what I will say now has to do with you also if you are a woman whose main occupation is studying. If you have received Christ as your Saviour, He sits in class with you, studies and takes examinations with you.

As in every other area of life, our attitude toward our

work is the key. You may or may not be in the work you would choose for yourself. And even if you are in your chosen field, as homemaker or career woman, I'm sure there are certain tasks connected with your work which you actively dislike.

This is simply because you are human. So don't kick yourself around for it.

But one glowing secret which I have learned (although I do not always practice what I have learned in this area) is that *all work* can and should be a sacrament to the Christian.

A major part of the time, my personal belongings, clothes, a few books, my portable phonograph, a small case of favorite recordings, my portable typewriter and file cabinet are either in the process of being packed or unpacked from the back of my automobile. Or in the process of being loaded or unloaded onto some redcap's dolly in a railroad station or airport. I hate to pack! And more than that, when I come home from a trip, I hate unpacking.

But when I remember that I can check toothpaste, makeup, cologne, writing paper, clean handkerchiefs and lingerie to the glory of God, the very thing I hate most becomes a sacramental effort. I am doing it for Him. I also wash dishes this way. It increases my sense of nearness to Him. It marks my thoughts indelibly with the certainty that there are no little things with God where I am concerned. He is interested in all of it. This knowing gives me an added experience of His love. And His love is the great transformer of our human personalities.

Anything that gives us a deeper conviction concerning the love of Christ is all glory! And there is no better place to find these tender indications of the true nature of His heart than in our work. Especially in the part of it which we happen to dislike. Anything that throws us onto Jesus Christ is something for which to give thanks.

Woman's work is one area of her life in which she can, if she will, and if she is seeing clearly, stay in an attitude of constant thanksgiving. My work gets too much for me most of the time. Writing books is the only part of it which I really enjoy. And other things have so crowded in that writing is almost the last thing I get around to doing. Speaking engagements, board meetings, writing short articles (which I don't enjoy!), telephone calls, troubled people, people with "great ideas" for religious TV and radio programs, TV and radio appearances, and the daily stack of mail to be answered—all this crowds my poor writing to the end of the list. And all I really *like* is the writing!

So, you see, I have much for which to be grateful. Every day I am thrown into some situation which forces me to remember that it can, it must (if I am to keep my sanity) be turned into a gesture of love on my part to the Lord Jesus Himself.

I am the first to admit, however, that *unless* He is, at the very moment of my feeling of being swamped, in full control of the very center of me, I am not even willing to make the unpleasant tasks a sacrament.

Please don't leap at the idea that I am complaining about my lot in life. I'd be as lonely as anyone else if no one wrote to me, and as discouraged as anyone else if the requests for speaking engagements suddenly stopped. I am thankful for all of it. But I am also human and like you, I have certain tasks which I enjoy naturally, and others which I must enjoy supernaturally.

I'm sure you follow me when I say that if there were only the daily forty or fifty letters, or only the new radio and TV ideas to work out, or only the speaking engagements, that would be different. If you only had the ironing to do today, or the shopping and the family chauffeuring, or if you had only your boss's current mail to get out, or if you only had your regular appointments to keep. If only. But life and work are not like that. No one's life and no one's work is truly simple.

All of it is beyond us if we are honest.

But none of it is beyond Jesus Christ.

And we have access to His poise and His patience and His clear insight and His wisdom in making emergency decisions. We have access to His strength when we are too weary to tackle one other thing.

Anyone, in any walk of life, who has really put this truth to the test knows that it is a fact. Not a pious theory.

One woman, a supervisor of nurses in a large hospital, is living proof of the difference a Christ-controlled inner self can make in one's work. When Alyce E. gave her life to Jesus Christ in her late forties one Sunday afternoon during the time I was speaking at Cannon Beach conference grounds in Oregon, she was a bad-tempered, rebellious, disillusioned woman. By her own admission, her reputation among the nurses with whom she worked was good only where her professional capabilities were concerned. Her temper flared and she possessed no mean knack for cutting people down with her blazing tongue. Her work was heavy and hard. But I sensed in her a deep, deep capacity for God. Certainly I sensed in her a deep need for Him. She sensed it, too, although her first step toward Him was taken with some reservations on her part. Now, Alyce will be the first to tell you that He never has any reservations on His part! She cracked the door to her heart just a little and He came in. Just as He said He would.

Life had not been easy on Alyce during her forty years. It has not been easy on her since she became a follower of Jesus Christ. But in the main *she* has been easy on life! I couldn't keep back a smile the day one of her nurses told me herself that everyone at the hospital was buzzing about the change in Miss E's disposition. She was always skillful as a technician. But as a supervisor, much of her actual work was with people. With the nurses under her and with the doctors. Several years have gone by since Alyce placed her personality under the control of Christ and He has held it. Real tragedy slashed across her heart recently as a result of a horrible automobile accident. But the inner controls held. Alyce E. is a peaceful woman inside. And her work, while it is still hard, with the same problems as before, has become creative. She does more for the reputation of Jesus Christ among those with whom she works now than a hundred books or a thousand sermons!

"We didn't even know she had such a nice smile," the young student nurse told me. "Now, we all like to do things for her to make her smile!"

Not only is Alyce E. easier to work with, her work has become easier on her, too.

The change in her personality has not been sudden. It seldom is. And it is still going on. But her heart has been steadily intentioned *toward* Christ. She "gets" Him. And He's got her.

Another close friend of mine, who is a professor of English Literature in a southern college, has been a devout Christian for most of her life. Recently, however, she confided in me that for the first two years as a professor, she just did not love her students. Especially the slow-witted ones who didn't move quickly and with what she considered proper intellectual agility, through the heavy classics she was endeavoring to teach to them. Her work began to be a hateful thing instead of the good, creative thing it should have been, considering her own extreme love of English literature. But instead of buckling under it and falling into a pit of discouragement, she knew Christ well enough to know He had an answer for it. On her knees one night by her bed, she asked

Him, with tears streaming down her face, to give her His love for those slow students whose personalities she didn't happen to like.

Did He give it to her?

Of course He did. She had to see her own need of it first, however, before He could give it to her. We simply won't take things we don't really want! At first, she justified her impatience with her students by saying they were too stupid to deserve patience. She was not being realistic and she was close enough to God to know it. He had to make her willing to love the slow students first. And then He poured His love through her to such an extent that although she is still considered the toughest prof on campus, she is without a doubt one of the most loved. A weekend retreat off campus is just no fun at all to the students now, unless my dear professor friend is along.

As far as her ability and knowledge of her subject were concerned, she was already outstanding as a teacher. Now she is successful in all aspects of her work, because more important than their grasp of English literature is the total personalities of those young people whom she teaches. She is taking Christlike, loving care of their total personalities now. And she is able to do it because *her* total personality is Christ-controlled.

So far, we have spoken of two career women. What of the homemaker? How is her work affected by her own personality?

One of the greatest, most authentic Christian women I know is my dear friend, Anna Mow, to whom I dedicated my book *Share My Pleasant Stones*. To know her now makes her story difficult to believe. But she has told it herself on my radio series "Visit With Genie," and perhaps you have heard it.

She was a missionary to India for many years, and before

her recent retirement, she taught for several years at Bethany Biblical Seminary in Chicago. But at heart, she is first a homemaker. And in her own words: "I used to watch women leave my house after I had counseled with them and as they left, I actually envied them the help they had so apparently received from God! They showed personality changes and I didn't. I did a lot of public speaking then, too, and I taught a Sunday school class. I said all the right things but I wasn't living them at home at all. The Holy Spirit used two sharp knives, wielded by my son and my husband to cut out the cancer of self-control within me."

Tears came to her kind eyes as she told me what her husband and son had said to her.

"Mother, why can't you be at home the way you are in church on Sunday?" This from her young son.

"Anna, what would the people back home in the church think if they could see you acting up this way around the house—you, a missionary they've sent out?" This from her usually quiet, philosophical, gentle husband.

Anna Mow went straight to God. And through a series of chastening periods; He was at last given the inner controls of her being. Her life for the past twenty years has been like a touch of Christ Himself on every person fortunate enough to know her.

I know I for one will never be able to express adequately my thanks to God because she is my friend.

I have just now (as I write this paragraph) spoken by telephone to another woman who is a close friend of mine and who has given me full permission to tell you about the way in which God controls her personality as a homemaker. I must tell you that I chose Kay Gieser as an illustration because I have been in her home, have seen the harmony come out of the normal chaos which occasionally hits the best run homes when there are three boys and a girl. I have never been in a more beautifully decorated home. The Gieser family did much of the work themselves on their new house and Kay's infallible color sense soothes my senses every time I visit there. There is imagination and excellent taste and above all, there is peace.

Her husband is a successful eye surgeon, and also a genuine Christian. And before I spoke with Kay by telephone just now, I checked with him about her general disposition around the house! He gave her a glowing recommendation.

And when I spoke with her, she was gracious enough to share with us the verse from the fifty-eighth chapter of Isaiah which is her refuge verse. I can see that it is more than a refuge. It is a stimulus to her to keep her conscious mind prodded into remembering that what it says can be true of her life and of her home. This is the verse she gave me: "And the Lord shall guide thee continually, and satisfy thy soul in drought, and make fat thy bones: and thou shalt be like a watered garden, and like a spring of water, whose waters fail not" (Isaiah 58:11).

Kay reminded me that some persons may still consider her a weed patch and not a watered garden! But this verse which shows the tremendous potential of her life as a homemaker linked with the life of Christ, is the pattern she follows.

She, of all people, knows that it is He who waters her garden. When her youngest boy, who is nine, and very, very talkative, gets too much for her, she asks him to excuse her a few minutes while she goes up to her room to talk to the Lord about things. This habit changes her and she usually finds the youngster changed, too, when she comes back downstairs. But most of her talking to the Lord is during dishes and cleaning and dusting. She teaches two Bible classes a week, does her own cooking and cleaning, and keeps herself, as well as her house, always attractive. She asked me to be sure to tell you that she finds discipline for herself as important (or maybe more so) as for her children. She quite agrees that we have to form the habit of remembering that this living water in the Person of the indwelling Christ is always available. Our discipline is to remember to keep our inner selves conscious of His presence. He never leaves. The water is always there. But we do forget about it. We do forget about Him. Especially when something is broken and two children are crying and the laundryman rings the doorbell and the laundry isn't gathered up yet. This is an excellent time to forget about the One who waters your garden. But He is still there. Waiting for you to remember Him.

Perhaps you are thinking, "Well, if my husband were a successful eye surgeon and I didn't have so many financial worries, I'd be a better homemaker, too!"

A good point. But the same principle applies. Nothing changes Jesus Christ. He is neither limited nor helped along by our circumstances.

Another friend of mine, in whose modest, but attractive home I lived for several days while speaking in her city, is equally as successful as Kay Gieser as a homemaker. Her name is Lethe Neeper and her personal life, her home, her disposition and her natural charm do great credit to Jesus Christ. In fact, Lethe and her husband and their three adopted children won my heart within the first five minutes after I arrived. I know of no one else who can meet and understand and show the love of Christ to her non-believing neighbors in a more convincing way than Lethe Neeper. She is not poor, but certainly she is not well-to-do. And it was an education to me to watch her coordinate her housework, laundry, meals, make a steady flow of contacts concerning my meetings and still stay casual and good-tempered with the active and inquisitive two small girls she has adopted.

Her delightful sense of humor is proof enough to me that Christ is in control of her personality!

As long as we are taking ourselves so seriously we cannot laugh when irritations pile up, it is a sure sign that we are not taking Him seriously enough. Lethe Neeper knows how to laugh. And she doesn't just laugh at a messy house and go on in spite of it. She could, if she had to, but her Christ-controlled personality gives her added energy, since little of it is wasted in complaining. I have sometimes cringed at the dripping, knotted disarray in some bathrooms when there are small children in the home. The whole Neeper family and I shared the same bath. I saw no confusion and no quick, frantic cleaning going on. It was a neat, orderly house. And even when the girls (aged two and four) dumped torn paper all over the living room rug two minutes before dinner one night, Lethe didn't lose her poise or humiliate the youngsters. There was no resentment evident from her, from her husband, from the little strewers or from their twelve-year-old brother. The whole family rallied around Lethe and the damage was cleaned up in no time. I sensed a loyalty to her because no one had cause to resent her.

She wasn't on her good behavior for me. She was natural. I would have sensed immediate resentment in the youngsters over the pre-dinner accident, if her normal way had been to shout at them. Lethe Neeper is not a perfect woman. Who is? But she impressed me greatly as having a Christ-controlled personality. For this reason her heavy church work, her heavy housework, her heavy responsibility of bringing up three children, her heavy concern that her neighbors know Jesus Christ, is carried on with a minimum of confusion.

Perhaps you hate housework and yet you got married a long time ago and now there are children and you feel trapped. You may be one of those well-meaning, but uneasy and inwardly rebellious women who feel she is "called" into full-time Christian work. Who feels her gifts are being wasted waxing floors and polishing windows and washing the same dishes over and over and over. Maybe you're a typist and you hate it. And you're also sure that you should be in full-time Christian work. Be sure your problem is not going to be neglected in this book. But it will be looked at in the chapter on rebellions. It belongs there.

Here, we have attempted to look at various women who work under varying conditions. We have tried to find out what Christ really has to do with their work and their attitudes toward it.

Everyone's work gets "too much" now and then. But I can't see that work is a curse upon the human race. I consider it a blessing. One of God's greatest. Neither do I believe we will sit around in heaven strumming harps on golden curbstones. I hope not. I'm sure I'd never learn to play a harp. And I think even in heaven we'd get tired of nothing but harp music! I believe there will be work in heaven. Good, creative work to keep us growing and to keep us learning.

In Mark's gospel is a much overlooked line which is the key to our working conditions on earth: "And they went forth . . . the Lord working with them."

Jesus Christ *wants* to work with us.

7

The Difference Christ Makes . . .

IN YOUR APPEARANCE

7

The Difference Christ Makes . . .

IN YOUR APPEARANCE

What difference does it make in a woman's appearance whether or not her personality is Christ-controlled?

I am well aware that what I have to say in this chapter will be cause for some criticism and some rejoicing. This is a subject which I have discussed with more women from all backgrounds, than any other subject.

If you do not agree with me in all that I have to say, please know that I fully respect your thinking and your right to it. And I trust you will do the same for me.

For a long time women have been asking me to write a book on how to lose weight. I admit, I did consider a separate book on the subject. However, it seems to fit the content of this one, so this is the chapter in which I will share my thinking and my methods of losing weight. At this writing I have lost a total of sixty pounds since my conversion. I need to lose about twenty more. Because of my heavy schedule, I have been advised by my doctor to do this quite slowly. I share these secrets with you so that you who are overweight, too, will know (in case you've never seen me!) that I am totally in this thing with you. I don't have to try to identify with you. I'm there.

But for those of you who need to count your blessings because you are not overweight, there will be much which will interest you here too. You may not agree with me, but if there is a woman who *pretends* she doesn't care about her appearance, then about her I'll have to say she is doing just that—pretending.

We will look at three aspects of a woman's appearance as we attempt to find out what Christ's control of her life really has to do with the way she looks.

First, *general grooming.*

Second, *adornment.*

Third, *weight.*

It is still unfortunately true that many of those outside the Christian world feel that Christians are people who couldn't make it any other way! Actually, they are quite right in the deepest sense. Christians are the relieved of this world who have *found out* about human helplessness and everyone's need for God. But, I'm afraid this is not quite what our non-believer friends see or look for. They see active Christians as probable social misfits. Strange, ungainly personalities who live depressed and depressing lives. Offbeat "characters," if you please, who have turned to religion as an escape. Or unattractive people who have taken refuge in their own shut-away world made up of other equally unattractive and peculiar individuals.

Much of this has been dispelled in the last ten years. It is a great deal easier to talk about Christ now than it was nine years ago when I was converted. But the general stigma still holds and I believe Christian women are somewhat to blame.

I well remember one conversation I had about the appearance of Christian women, with the friend who led me to Christ. She made her first inroad in His behalf upon my consciousness by the very fact that she was well dressed, carefully groomed and altogether smart looking. We were on the subject (or I was!) of my girlhood memories of the "devout." My mother was always well dressed and she was a Christian, but to my mind, she must have been special. I remember saying to my friend, "You don't figure. You can't believe all you say you believe because you don't look the part. Your slip doesn't show!"

Ruth and Billy Graham have done more to dispel this myth about Christians not being normal people than perhaps any other Christian couple because they are both so much publicized and because they are both so attractive and well groomed. And I believe our appearance as Christians is as great a responsibility as any other.

Jesus Christ has brought a great amount of order into a world still only partially Christianized. Where His touch is felt upon a nation, that nation is far ahead in sanitation, conservation of natural resources and orderly government. He is not the author of maladjustment. When a woman's twisted personality is straightened out, so will be the seams in her stockings and the part in her hair! He is interested in the total personality and this certainly includes our looks as well as our insight.

Grooming

I feel it is my Christian duty to be at least as careful in my personal grooming, if not more so, than before my conversion. You may have dry hair and my habits may not be workable for you. But shampooing my hair twice a week is as much a part of my spiritual life as my daily quiet time.

A Christian woman in a baggy skirt and a blouse that isn't fresh is a bad witness, no matter what else she does. If you can't afford frequent dry cleaning bills, then buy clothing which is washable. If you can't go to the hairdresser often, then have your hair styled so you can handle it yourself. I don't visit my hairdresser once between permanents. She has styled my hair so that I can shampoo and set it myself without benefit of one single bobby pin!

Americans have been accused of overbathing. Sometimes when I am pressed into the middle of a crowd of people after a meeting, I think this is an unjust accusation! I think I'm too tired for a shower sometimes, too, but I always feel rested and refreshed after I take it. Just the nervous tension alone in the average twentieth century woman's life is adequate reason for a daily bath. And if your best friend won't tell you, I'll tell you that there are excellent deodorants on the market. And they are not on the market to keep TV stations in operation, they are on the market for us to use —regularly. Women, I must say, are not as adept at offending in this way as men. At least this has been my experience in crowds. But we all need to remember, as Christians, that we not only "present our bodies" unto the Lord, we present them to those who don't yet know Him, too! No matter how many Bible verses you can quote, no matter how well you have all your points assembled for winning a person to Jesus Christ, if you offend that person's finer senses, you may slam the door of the Kingdom in his or her face.

A few good poems and thousands of bad ones have been written about a woman's hands. About the touch of a woman. It can be a soothing, creative experience. Or it can feel like a brush with a piece of number two sandpaper. I know all about detergents in the dishpan. No wonder they cut grease on dishes and skillets so quickly, look what they do to the natural oils in our hands! Mine show it immediately. But, no reason to blame detergents. Make more frequent use of your hand lotion. Keep a bottle at the kitchen sink and keep using it. I know what housework and packing and unpacking heavy suitcases from a car can do to fingernails, too. But this is no excuse for poorly groomed nails on a woman's hands. Any leading manufacturer of nail polish also manufactures nail cream. And the ads are true which claim that extra-heavy portions of protein in gelatin form prevent breaking nails. Typing as much as I do, I am speaking from experience when I speak of broken nails.

My eyes go involuntarily to two points of a woman's anatomy when I meet her. Her hands and her teeth. Glamorous, long, regularly formed nails and white even rows of teeth are found only rarely except in the ads for toothpaste and nail polish. But teeth can be clean and nails can be clean and both can, and must be, regularly cared for if we are to be good for the reputation of Jesus Christ in our daily contacts.

Quite sometime ago I learned that after thirty minutes of talking, the human throat dries out to such an extent that the breath is bad as a consequence. As regular a part of the mysterious contents of my purse as a comb, is a bottle of breath sweetener or a roll of mints. No one is safe from offending in this way. The slightest tip one way or another in our body chemistry, from fatigue, overeating, or overtalking can cause halitosis. And quite often lack of proper dental care causes it. The use of dental floss and a rubber massage tip on your toothbrush will help wonderfully.

I am very much aware that you already know these things. I am not writing this book for bush women. I am writing it for you. And I am writing as I am in this chapter more as a reminder that we owe careful grooming to the Lord as part of obedience. Polish your shoes, clean your galoshes, shampoo your hair, care for your skin and nails and teeth, and bathe frequently to the glory of God! All of these things, too, can be meaningful sacraments if we really love Christ.

Adornment

I am marching now, right into what some of you may not even know is a battlefield among women. Christian women, that is. I know I am suspect with many groups and will be more so, no doubt, because of what I am going to say here about woman's *adornment* if she is a Christian.

And before I begin to say it, I want you to know that I know the particular verses in the Bible which many sincere people feel prohibit a Christian woman from adorning herself at all. I fully respect this thinking. I respect the willingness of these persons to be "different." Being different isn't an easy thing for most of us. And I also want to express in print my gratitude to the dozen or more people who have written to me (a few quite kindly!) about the fact that I do use a moderate amount of make-up and I do wear small earrings and I do occasionally wear a ring. I am well aware that my critics are oftentimes the unpaid guardians of my soul. And I pray about every letter that comes, in which I am criticized for any reason.

I am thinking now of several genuine Christian women whom I love and whose lives show their love of Christ. These women don't wear make-up at all. Some never have. Others have gotten "guidance" to stop wearing it. This "guidance" I respect deeply. I simply have never gotten it. In no way do I intend this to be an argument for wearing make-up and jewelry as a Christian. I am stating my beliefs and my reasons for holding them. You are free to take them or leave them. One dear friend of mine, who feels "led" not to wear earrings herself, had humor enough to send me a lovely pair for my birthday last year! Women are a strange lot. On this the men will agree. And I think we should, too. With our humors in full operation.

Most of the persons who write to me (kindly or unkindly)

quote Peter on the subject. I have before me as I write two translations of I Peter 3:3, 4. One is the King James translation and the other is the contemporary and fine Berkeley translation. Here they are:

King James: "Whose adorning let it not be that outward adorning of plaiting the hair, and of wearing of gold, or of putting on of apparel; But let it be the hidden man of the heart, in that which is not corruptible, even the ornament of a meek and quiet spirit, which is in the sight of God of great price."

Berkeley: "Your adornment should not be on the outside—braided hair, putting on gold trinkets, or wearing attractive dresses; *instead*, the inner personality of the heart with the imperishable qualities of a gentle and quiet spirit, something of surpassing value in God's sight."

The italics used in printing the word "instead" in the Berkeley version are mine. This, to me, is the key. It is not so clearly said in the King James version, but it is still there in meaning. In other words, this does not necessarily mean that women are not to adorn themselves at all. As I see it, and as many other Christians see it (including Dr. Verkuyl who edited the Berkeley version), it simply means that our most noticeable adornment as Christian women must be *inward!* If my make-up and jewelry and extremely cut clothes call more attention to me outwardly than does my Christian spirit, then I am wrong.

Christians of either sex are not to call attention to themselves primarily. Jesus Christ lived a normal, unobtrusive life on earth. He dressed the way other people dressed. He did not make eccentric use of His religion. He moved easily and naturally among the people whom He had come to save. He did not draw away from them at all. He did not compromise His holiness for one minute, but neither did He do anything that made Him appear odd or peculiar.

At the time of my conversion, I wore much too much make-up. Heavy, overdrawn mouth, eye shadow, mascara, and very, very dark pancake make-up on my face. No one told me to stop. My heart just wasn't in calling attention to me any longer. I toned it all down. Way down. I'm not against discriminate use of it, but I have large eyes and didn't really need eye shadow anyway, so I dropped that altogether. All excess seemed to drop away. And for the first time in my entire life I found myself hating to call attention to me. This, in fact, was one of the first strong inner impulses which the Lord used in convicting me because I was so much overweight. Overweight women call attention to themselves. Heavily made-up women call attention to themselves. Women dripping with large, glassy jewelry call attention to themselves. And, by the same token, in the twentieth century, women devoid of any color in their faces also call attention to themselves.

It is the inner life which must glow and attract. Dr. Verkuyl, in one of his excellent footnotes in the Berkeley translation says of the oft-quoted I Peter 3:3, 4: "(Adornments) not forbidden; Sara and Rebekah wore them; but minor in comparison with Christian character traits."

I want to say once more, however, that no one should take my word for this. For that matter, not even Dr. Verkuyl's. Go to the Lord. And if you honestly believe He is telling you to leave off all adornment, then by all means leave it off. Some women in certain groups seem to feel that it is all right to wear jeweled pins, but not earrings. Others that it is all right to wear necklaces, but not earrings. Earrings have it hard. Why, I don't know. They're usually made up about the same as necklaces and brooches, but they are much discriminated against in certain groups. There are even some who feel they should not wear their wedding rings. This, too, is a personal matter. But Jesus apparently didn't disapprove of rings. In the prodigal son story (which Jesus made up) He is attempting to show us what the Father's heart is really like. Attempting to convince us that our heavenly Father is capable of making merry when one of His loved ones comes home. And one of the ways in which He illustrates this point is to say that the father in the story called to his servants ordering them to "put a ring on his finger." But again, I am not arguing for the wearing of jewelry or any other adornment. I am simply attempting to force us as women to look at what the Bible says is the *central issue:* our very inner natures themselves. Let not your main adornment be outward—let it be inward.

One well-meaning and devout Christian gentleman wrote to me several years ago telling me that my Christian witness would be much more forceful if I stopped wearing lipstick at all. I didn't get into a discussion with him. I simply thanked him and left it there. But *to whom* would it be more forceful? At the time he wrote that letter I was directing a dramatic radio program on which I hired professional actors and actresses all of whom had known me in my old life. They all knew, straight from my own lips, that I had given my life to Jesus Christ. Seven of them became followers as a result of their contacts with us on that program. But, speaking from my own knowledge of myself as I was before my conversion, I, had I been in their places, would have thought me excessively queer if I had suddenly turned up for rehearsal sans any color at all.

I believe God guides us on these things according to the particular people to whom He has sent us. This may appear to be unscriptural to many. But He did say that we were to go into *all* the world. And much of the world today is frightened by peculiarities in human personality and appearance. I long to be made a truly natural person. I long to make identification wherever I can without compromising the holiness of the One who died for all of the so-called shocking people in the world.

Within the bounds of what I know of God's holiness I want to "be all things to all men." He has made me want to embrace the world and love it into loving Him. He has knocked down exclusive barrier after exclusive barrier in my personality. He has made me care, painfully at times, about those who are downright afraid of so-called religiosos! Afraid of church people. Afraid of their strange exclusive language. Afraid of their peculiarities. After all, Jesus was called a "glutton and a wine-bibber." I have no question whatever in my mind about His overeating or overdrinking. But He evidently spent His time with the people who did: They were the ones who needed Him.

After nine long years, I have at last discovered *how* to be with some of my old friends and still remain loyal to Christ. And now that I have gotten off my "don't touch me, I'm holy" pedestal and am just another human being again, they are more and more interested in knowing this Jesus Christ whom I love. And who loves and longs over them with all His great heart.

As for jewelry, I don't happen to care for the current trend in large, flashy stones. My ears are so funny I can't wear large earrings even if I liked them. I still prefer what I have always preferred, a few pieces of fairly good, but small, jewelry. This is no virtue. It is just my taste. Thanks to a few generous friends and my mother, I now own some nice pieces. But they are conspicuous only to those who can recognize the difference between junk and nicely made jewelry.

Genuine good taste has to stem from God! After all, He is the one who had the infinite good taste to create crocuses, rainbows, small orchids and green ocean waves at sunset. All real beauty is His. And He will guide you. He knows where He has placed you and with whom.

And once again, the whole matter hinges on the one often repeated baseline of this entire book: Is your personality Christ-controlled?

Weight

To those of you who are so strangely created that you can eat all you want to eat of anything without adding pounds, I will only repeat: Count your blessings. But I think you had better tag along with us through this section of this chapter simply because many of you are just fortunate. Not necessarily more spiritual than the rest of us whose every mouthful seems to lodge, not inside, but outside our stomachs!

My dear friend, Ellen Urquhart, with whom I lived for eight years before her recent marriage, once gained ten pounds during an illness. Her lifelong weight had shattered the scales at a wicked one hundred pounds. Suddenly she could no longer get into her clothes. And she joined me for one month on my usual diet. In the joining, she found in herself deep, otherwise hidden rebellions. Food became so important to her, she set our dinner hour up to 4:30 P.M.! Bright and early every morning she was up teeming for breakfast. And, being a genuine Christian, she saw that she had been guilty all her life, not only of pride in her figure, but of spiritual pride because she wasn't overweight!

To those of us who are overweight, the same principle applies. But we have an extra hurdle to overcome. We must overcome our rebellion at being put together metabolically as we are. There is nothing accomplished whatever by complaining bitterly that your husband can "eat like a horse and stay thin as a rail." If you can't, then just proceed from there.

In losing weight, acceptance of yourself as you are, is the first and probably the most important thing of all. Remember, during the losing of my sixty pounds, I was living with Ellen who weighed (except for that brief month) one hundred pounds. And stayed that way, even though she sat across the table from me eating large spoons of mayonnaise and piles of whipped cream. I, on the other hand, sat on the other side of the table eating diet mayonnaise or vinegar and Sucaryl and limiting myself to one glass of skimmed milk a day. She ate ice cream while I ate yogurt, artificially sweetened and mixed with unsweetened canned grapefruit.

As long as I stayed at home in Chicago, my excess poundage slipped gradually away. When I traveled, some of it invariably went back on. Until I began staying in hotels and motels and eating my meals alone, under doctor's orders, to protect my voice. When I did that, I found that I continued to shed the pounds. Why? Because I was no longer being entertained in the homes of Christians.

Before I say more, let me make it clear that much of the joy of my Christian life, especially back in the first years, when I still felt somewhat strange among you, came from the warm love and hospitality which you showed me in caring for my every need. I thank you from my heart.

But here is an interesting fact. Only three times in all the years in which I have been dined in the homes of Christians, and especially during those after-meeting fellowship hours, have I ever been served a dessert that was not literally packed with calories! Now, don't get the idea that I didn't thoroughly enjoy the hundreds of other meals. Why do you think I'm overweight? I enjoy eating. I am a gourmet by nature. But the interesting fact which has struck me is that with rare exception, we as Christians seem to be trying to compensate for some of the so-called taboo pleasures of the world at our dining room tables; and on top of that we thank the Lord profusely before we do it!

Instead of overdrinking or oversmoking, we are overstuffing. And gluttony is listed in one of Paul's careful lists of sins.

My brother, Joe, who had been far overweight all his life, suddenly came to himself after his conversion, and in order to qualify for a certain fine position which he felt God had sent to him, got busy and lost seventy-eight pounds in six months. This is too fast for good health, but he got the job. And he has held his weight with no variation beyond four or five pounds one way or the other for five years. It so happens that he is still smoking. And some of the people in his church give him a bit of a rough time over it. His rare sense of humor and his inherited outspokenness and what I believe to be his genuine Christian character hold him in these times of criticism because he still smokes. He knows the people are praying for him and he is grateful. But the people who pray regularly for him to "straighten up" are at least fifty or more pounds overweight!

Joe looks them in the eye, smiles broadly, and says: "When you lose some weight, come back and we'll talk." He is a comparatively new Christian. His accusers have known the Lord for many years.

Excessive smoking is harmful to the human body. But no more harmful (and I have checked with doctors on this) than overeating! If you and I are overweight, we have absolutely no right to disapprove of someone else's smoking or dressing this way or that.

Not once has the Lord given me peace about my size. I have come down from a twenty to a sixteen, but as one perceptive friend said to me not long ago, "You can't justify yourself on how much you've already lost. You can only afford to get busy on what there is still left to lose!"

And she is dead right.

Now, how do we do this? Where does Christ come into the picture?

I had thought of including some of my favorite diet dinner menus. But these are so accessible to everyone that I will just recommend two excellent books to you and then speak of the underlying principles involved. If you purchase and read and follow the reducing plans in either of these well-known books, you will lose the weight you need to lose:

(1) *Eat Well and Stay Well,* by Ancel and Margaret Keys (Doubleday).
(2) *New Guide to Intelligent Reducing,* By Gayelord Hauser (Farrar, Straus & Young).

Of course, no one should attempt a rigid diet without a doctor's examination. I am under a doctor's care for the first time in my life right now. I am one of those disgustingly healthy creatures who has darkened a doctor's office only once before in her whole life. But I am serious about reducing my size and since my body belongs to Christ, I mean to do it intelligently. And so I am regularly visiting a doctor who specializes in weight reduction. He keeps check on my blood pressure (which tends to be high) and my heart. He also keeps check on the inches I have or have not lost! And this helps, too.

On my doctor's recommendation, my breakfast is always two raw eggs beaten in a glass of orange or pineapple juice, and black coffee. The idea of raw eggs sickened me, too, at first. Now, I find I never tire of it! Unless I add plenty of artificial sweetener (such as liquid Sucaryl) I can't take it. But when I do, I love every drop.

If you think you can't drink black coffee, put a dash of skimmed milk in it for the love of Jesus Christ. Just a couple of days of coffee with skimmed milk and you'll like it just as well as that fat-filled cream you've been using.

For lunch I major on cottage cheese and yogurt. All I want. Many people hate the thought of yogurt. And alone, it is sharp and unappetizing. But mix equal portions of cottage cheese with it, add some fresh or unsweetened canned fruit (a small amount—remember fruit is full of sugar!), more liquid sweetener, stir it up and I promise it will satisfy that emotional urge for gooey sweet things! It is creamy and delicious. But don't forget the liquid sweetener to your taste.

Fortunately for both of us, my new associate, Rosalind Rinker, also fights the familiar battle of the bulge. When we are at home and most of the time when we are traveling, we stick to this raw eggs, yogurt and cottage cheese ritual all day until dinner. I mention Rosalind to shake any possible idea which you might have that I must be peculiar or I couldn't eat this way. She loves it, too.

Buy a copy of one of the two books I have mentioned, or any good reducing diet book for your evening meal. And if you have followed my diet all day every day, you will find that your appetite for overrich food for dinner has greatly diminished.

But the glorious open secret which I have learned is that when we are doing this for love's sake, it is not hard! I am losing weight for Jesus Christ's sake. I want to be good for His reputation and I feel I would do equal damage to it if I walked on a platform smoking a cigarette or if I waddled onto a platform hauling along a shameful excess of ugly poundage. I know of only one overweight woman whose extra pounds are directly traceable to a strange, incurable glandular unbalance. There are a few others, I'm sure. I want them to know I am not speaking to them in these pages. I am speaking to the rest of us who *can* lose our excess baggage and glorify Jesus Christ if we choose to.

There are three spiritual exercises involved:

(1) We must *accept* ourselves as we are. We must stop pitying us by a continual wondering, "Why it is that every bite I put into my mouth goes to fat!" If we remain in this attitude, we are secretly blaming God for creating us as He did. We may not admit it, but it's true. And as long as we resent Him, even subconsciously, we will not be able to do the next thing. We must know Him and we must love Him. Not a whipped up "love" that stands up long enough for a public testimony or a declaration of Biblical doctrine. But a love strong enough to make sacrifices for His sake when no one is looking.

(2) We must be *willing* to begin making these sacrifices. He has given us all "choosers." Our part is to use them. I have never lost weight on a diet I started tomorrow. The only time I've ever been able to lose weight is to choose to start now.

(3) *The love-offering.* Make a list of all the rich foods you love with an unholy passion! The list is necessary only in nailing down your determination. So much has been written about caloric content of food, no one really needs to do any research here. The spiritual point is this: When you bake a cake or a pie, or when dessert is passed at a dinner or a banquet, *smile* and say, "No, thank you." It's really just as easy to say as, "Yes, thank you." *And in your heart, right at that moment, make a picture of yourself handing that rich dessert or that bowl of mashed potatoes or that homemade roll directly to the Lord as a love-offering!*

When we deprive ourselves of something we love, we feel put upon. But when we *give* something we love to Someone we love, it is a different thing. I can promise you this will work. It has worked sixty pounds worth for me and I expect it to work for the remaining twenty.

This, I assure you, is much easier to do in public when there are people around to impress. And those of you who are homemakers have a difficult problem here. But the answer, once more, is spiritual in nature. Is Jesus Christ real to you?

Are you convinced that He meant what He said when He said, "Lo, I am with you alway?" If you are, then half the battle is won of an afternoon in your kitchen when no human being would know if you sneaked a piece of mince pie! Jesus will know. He is there. And it is for Him that you are doing this anyway, isn't it?

Does it make a difference in a woman's appearance whether or not her personality is Christ-controlled? Yes. And He is not an eccentric. He wants us to look our best. I believe we are responsible for what our faces and our bodies *say* to those whom we meet, particularly after we are thirty-five. We can't all be cover girls. But our outward appearance is again only a manifestation of what is truly inside us.

A woman's grooming, her adornment, her size are definite indications of who is at the controls of her life.

Is Jesus Christ at the controls of your life?

Or are you?

8

The Difference Christ Makes . . .
IN YOUR MARRIED LIFE

8

The Difference Christ Makes ...

IN YOUR MARRIED LIFE

Does it make a real difference in a woman's relationship with her husband whether or not her life is controlled by Jesus Christ?

Perhaps some may think I, a single woman, would have little to say about this. But human relationships are all basically the same, and I will be drawing heavily in this chapter on actual stories about women and their husbands whom I know personally.

I would like to say that the statistics about divorce which shock most people don't shock me at all. I am amazed that so few marriages end in the divorce courts! Real harmony is necessary for two people of opposite sex to live together under one roof. And according to Webster, harmony is "a just adaptation of parts to each other."

How many of us are *really willing* to adjust to someone else? Particularly in the case of marriage when the courtship has been built on the timeworn, but still popular method of the gentleman in the case paying gallant court to the lady in the case. Often, he tells her she is beautiful. Often, he brings her little gifts. He opens doors for her and carries her books or bundles. He is not only expected to wait for her to "complete" herself, but he is expected to exclaim enthusiastically about the results of her efforts to make herself beautiful.

Nothing can be done about the expected flattering and extravagant build-up which the average male gives to the average female during the days preceding the honeymoon. This is custom and tradition and it is his inherent nature to do it, and her inherent nature to expect it.

Then they are married. He is busy and forgets. He is tired and doesn't notice the new dress. She is busy and occasionally forgets to repair her lipstick or comb her hair before he comes home, the conquering hero from his day's labor. He doesn't compliment her enough any more and she doesn't do much to deserve it.

The more emotionally unstable of the two begins to quake inwardly about the honeymoon being over and the very rafters of the love-nest scream for "adjustment!"

Harmony.

It would be a horrible and chaotic world if honeymoons did last. On honeymoons, I am told, the lovers have only eyes and ears and minds for each other. If all married people remained in this introverted state, who would keep the stores open, who would preach the sermons, who would run the banks, who would operate the bakeries and the beauty salons, and who would practice medicine, try legal cases and repair automobiles? For that matter, not only the gentlemen would be immobilized where society is concerned, but so would the ladies. Who would wash the dishes and type the letters and mend the clothes and teach politeness and instill emotional stability in the little tousled dears who would keep resulting from the perpetual honeymoon?

The whole brain-smashing complexity of marital relations has not been adequately covered yet in all the slick magazine articles and heavy tomes expounding it. And certainly, we can do no more than be honest about some of the basic problems in this one chapter. But I shall attempt to reveal something of what I have seen happen and something of what I have learned firsthand from the hundreds of women with whom I have discussed this important relationship.

And we will, of course, be primarily concerned with the fact that if God created the marriage relationship, certainly He is capable of making it work. Provided at least someone involved is willing to live a Christ-controlled life. The statistics on the divorce rate among active Christians are low. This would indicate that Christian couples have a way of meeting and solving their difficulties. They still have them, but they have a way out, too. However, I believe we must be altogether realistic. All Christian married couples are not well adjusted, happy people. Here again, from having stayed in so many Christian homes during the past several years, I have unconsciously developed another kind of antenna. I can tell rather quickly whether or not there is real love and real peace between Mr. and Mrs. Evangelical. Christ *is* the way out of marital problems, but some don't seem to know how to appropriate Him. Some Christian couples stay married simply because they don't believe in divorce.

One thing sure, we can't solve the husbands' personality problems for them, but we can consider honestly some of the adjustments which Christian women have to face. And if you are not a Christian, we who are hope that our honesty in admitting our need for Christ in every relationship will help to convince you of your need for Him, too.

I have chosen to divide this chapter according to the marital problems about which women talk to me most frequently.

(1) *"My husband seems to be jealous of our children."*
This would seem to indicate a decidedly selfish streak in Mr.
Husband. I have discovered from actual contacts and from
my reading on the subject that this is not necessarily true
at all. It is certainly true that children do take more of a
woman's attention. They require more of her time. They
have a special hold on her heart. And without a doubt, the
mother has more of a dual role to play than her husband.
She is with the children most of the time. They are an integral part of her work, just as the husband's customers or
clients or patients are an integral part of his work. And
coming home, to the husband, means freedom from these
work contacts. He is in a different atmosphere altogether.
He can get away from his work much more easily than a
woman, who never really gets away from hers! She may love
her little "customers" with all her heart, but they are always
around. Needing her.

I am thinking, as I write, of one young mother whose
heart was broken and whose faith in God was really shaken.
Her husband had begun to stay at the office at night. She
had no real reason to suspect him of anything more than
staying at the office, but she was sinking rapidly into the
mud of self-pity and making more mud for herself by shed-
ding copious tears over the fact that her husband didn't love
her any more.

After another slight torrent or two of weeping, we got
down to facts. They had had their first real argument when
he came home one evening all excited about an ice show in
town. He had tickets and wanted to take his wife out on a
real date, replete with orchids and dinner in the best restaurant. He was being a thoughtful husband. He wasn't doing
it all for her, though, because I'm convinced from other
things she told me that he wanted to do it for his own
heart's sake, too. He was proud of the way she looked and

he longed to recapture some of the fun they had together before the baby came.

A little more investigation on my part and I discovered that their three-year-old child had begun to cry noisily the moment her mother said: "But, darling, I can't leave Nancy! You remember how she cried and cried the last time we left her with the baby sitter."

Nancy's three-year-old ears caught the phrase "I can't leave Nancy." This was her little cue. And she took it lustily.

Nancy won. They didn't go. And the incident had been repeated several times within the year. Only once did the wife agree to go out with her husband alone. Night after night they sat at home, while Nancy turned rapidly into a spoiled brat who knew all she had to do was begin to make loud use of the favorite weapon of her sex—tears. Night after night they sat at home, and then night after night the confused, foolish wife began baby sitting alone.

You who are mothers may honestly think you are doing the best thing for your children when you put them first. You are not. Your husband must be given equal billing with them. He may be ever so proud a father, and he no doubt loves the children as much as you do, but he loves you, too. And if you are going to give your youngsters the security which they need so desperately in childhood, you must keep the love between you and your husband alive. Show him affection before them. A family unselfconscious about kissing one another is a basically happy family. I shall always be glad for this in my own childhood. I kissed my mother every morning before I went to school. So did my brother. And he also kissed me. Dad drove me to school and it didn't even occur to me to be shy about giving him a kiss before I hopped out of the car. He and Mother kissed every time they parted right up to their last parting the afternoon of the day he went to be with the Lord.

Your children will feel an insecurity impossible to describe if they cannot count on the love mother has for dad and the love dad has for mother. This, of course, is the reason why youngsters from broken homes are marked permanently by a deep, dark sense of dread that crawls and claws under every phase of their lives. The child has a right for his parents to love each other. They are his only security. They are the rock *or* the quicksand under his first steps into adulthood.

It seems rather generally to be a woman's instinct to be a protective mother. Not always, but generally. It also seems to be her instinct to be a spoiled brat where her husband is concerned. But from my concrete observations, I am convinced that if you are a good wife, you will also be a good mother. You cannot be a good mother unless you are a good wife first. If you are not considerate of your husband, you will knock from beneath your child the very thing he wants most—security.

The next time your husband asks you to go out, go. And if he has gotten out of the habit, ask him to take you! It may take a few invitations on your part before he gets back into his chivalrous ways again, but persevere. For his sake. For the children's sake. For your own sake and for Christ's sake.

(2) *"My husband is so demanding of me. He expects too much of me physically and socially. I can't keep up with him. Women just don't have as much energy as men."*

There are exceptions to all generalities. But again from many, many talks with women (and not a few with their husbands, too) I am convinced that most "demanding" husbands are, at heart, disappointed little boys. I agree that a demanding mate is an immature mate. But could it be that his wife is the instigator of this strange, new side of his personality which appeared after married life settled down into the daily thing it is?

What happens in your house when your husband comes home? The masculine ego is something which all women who marry men should take into consideration. There it is. It is a part of the reason he is a man. It is not his nature to work quietly behind the scenes. The responsibility of providing for you and your children are his. And ego is not a sinful trait, unless it is inflated. It is, in reality, our identity. You have an ego, too. That's what suffers when he neglects you. If he has become demanding, it is because he is suffering, too. Maybe his own mother failed to encourage him. Maybe he was suffering from the same feeling of inadequacy when you married him. Maybe it only started to show recently.

Whatever the cause, do you (honestly, now) encourage him enough? Are you willing to stop for just one minute when he comes home to give him a welcoming kiss and ask him about his day? And after you ask him, do you remember to listen to what he has to say, or do you run back to the kitchen as though you hadn't asked a thing? Men need to be built up by the women they love. This isn't flattery. There must be something about him you admire or you wouldn't have married him in the first place. Let him know you still admire it.

If your husband is demanding, there is at least a strong possibility that you have forgotten that he needs attention, too. He is demanding it. It is his right. And if he makes his demands in an ungentlemanly way, that is only because he isn't perfect any more than you are. Husbands need proof of love from their wives. Just as wives need proof of love from their husbands. Just because he invades your workshop at dinner time, don't treat him like an invader. It's his home, too.

(3) *"My husband is a social misfit (or a gambler, or a lazy ne'er-do-well, or an alcoholic). We just don't have anything in common."*

This complaint from women almost invariably comes from a woman who rushed into her marriage. More often than not, she is intellectually her husband's superior. Socially, she knows what to do, but he doesn't. And he humiliates her in public by talking too loudly or telling off-color jokes or by drinking. She has given up trying to go places with him. They are just together because of the children. Poor children!

I admit, these cases seem almost hopeless. How can a man's social or intellectual or sensitivity pattern be changed when he is an adult? Much of it can't be. Much of it won't be. But in a few instances, I have seen the wife change so much that a compatible relationship resulted in spite of the husband's personality defects. Actually, I have seen some changes in the husband himself, *once the wife did what every human being has to do with every other human being before any real harmony can result.*

She must *accept* him as he is!

One woman said to me that it took her twelve years to get to the place of accepting her husband as being an alcoholic who couldn't hold a job. "I couldn't get it out of my mind that my sister's husband was such a wonderful fellow. Why was mine the way he was?"

Finally, she began to see the great Christian wisdom in acceptance. God died on a Cross for us *as we are.* He does not demand that we "mend our ways." He takes us now and He died for us then, just exactly as we are. If we are followers of Jesus Christ, we must follow His thinking, too. And His actions.

Many men are driven deeper into their faults and sins and personality defects and social inadequacies by women who refuse to accept them as they are. But who also refuse to stop trying to change them. We can influence people, but only God, through His Holy Spirit, can change them.

The woman who had tried for twelve years to accept her

husband, is now, slowly, very slowly, but gradually creating in him an interest in life again. And an interest in life is just a step away from full acceptance of Life through Jesus Christ.

(4) *"My husband leaves all the disciplining of our children to me. I'm afraid the children will build up resentment toward me and just think their dad's tops."*

There could be many reasons why a father will do this. He could be so eager for his children's acceptance and approval that he leaves all the unpleasantness to his wife unconsciously. He could just be a weak character. He could be too busy. (A mistake on his part, but an explanation nevertheless.) He could hold some hidden resentment toward his wife, choosing to put her in a "bad light" with the children.

But we have said we cannot solve the gentlemen's difficulties. We can only go as far as possible, woman to woman, in facing our own. Could it be that you have not spoken highly enough in the past to your children of your husband's character? Children usually think of their father what mother thinks of him! Could it be that you have gone ahead with the discipline, allowing the child to know that you're doing it on your own without consulting their father? I realize that most of the actual disciplining of a child occurs when dad is at the office or the store or the factory. But it is always possible to include him, even though he isn't there. "Your father and I have talked this over." But be sure you have talked it over. If you draw your husband intelligently into things at home, he won't resent it. He'll be honored. And he should share the disciplinary measures with you. Give your youngsters the certainty that *you* respect their father's word and then they will come to respect it, too.

(5) *"My husband is a Christian. At least I think he is. But*

he isn't interested in my prayer groups and he won't read the Bible with me, etc."

This is a common problem. And I honestly believe that in many instances if the wife would *include* her husband more and stop fidgeting because he doesn't talk as much about his Christianity as she does, he might relax a little in it. Men are not talkative by nature (most of them). Your husband may have the seed of a living faith down in his heart, but you can jump up and down on it with anxiety and "spiritual talk" until it is buried so deeply he may think it is dead!

Here again, there are always exceptions. But if there is a spark of the life of Christ in him, cultivation is what it needs. And since the way to a man's heart is through his stomach, maybe you'll have to begin with his stomach! No woman can convince her husband of Christianity until she has convinced him of her love and respect for him as a person. Why not be simple and direct and natural with him where spiritual matters are concerned? Ask the Lord to open the way for such a conversation and tell your husband quite honestly (and as sweetly as you know how) that even though you feel you know what you believe about Jesus Christ, you would really be interested to know what he believes, too.

The way for such a conversation may be years in opening up (God and God alone knows when a heart is prepared), but in the meantime, let the man know you love him no matter what he believes!

(6) *"My husband is not a Christian and he is antagonistic about Christianity. He doesn't even want me to take our children to Sunday school. He says he wants them to be allowed to make their own decisions. And he wants me to keep still about religion around the house."*

This is perhaps the most common complaint of all. And

it is a difficult situation. But not a hopeless one. Nothing is hopeless when Jesus Christ is on the scene!

First of all, such a wife must *accept* her husband as he is: A non-believer. She must stop expecting him to be interested in something which he does not see. She must stop pitying herself for this state of affairs. She doesn't want her husband to become a Christian half so much as Jesus Christ wants him. In any relationship between a Christian and a non-Christian, the Christian must *always* remember that God created all people. And in them all, He created the need and the desire to belong to Himself. In every human being, even the most antagonistic, Jesus Christ has a hidden ally. This ally may be buried so deep within the person it is never noticeable. But it is there.

The wife with the non-Christian husband must proceed with this knowledge firmly in mind. She is not alone. God Himself is working. Her problem is to cooperate. He is never blind to the quirks of any personality. We often are. This wife must not ask God to help *her,* she must ask Him how she can better enable Him to *work through her!*

One woman asked me if I thought she should go to church every Sunday regardless of the fact that it always created an argument when she came home. Here again there is no pat answer. Many women go no matter what happens and in the going against opposition, they shift their intended Christ-like attitude to one of self-pity and develop an entirely unChristian persecution complex. This makes their Christianity even more unattractive to their husbands.

After prayer with her, I once suggested to a woman in this predicament that she be more direct with her husband. I suggested that she appeal to his reason—not about religion, but about the fairness of the thing. She tried it. She told her husband that she knew he had great respect for anyone with genuine convictions, political, social or otherwise. He agreed that he did. "I'm not trying to shove anything down your throat, honey," she went on, "I won't even ask you to go to church with me again. Not ever. But don't you respect my right to do what I honestly feel in my heart I should do?"

He agreed that he did.

"Well, why not think of my hour at church on Sunday as I think of the two evenings you are away bowling and working at the store? You feel you need to do both of them. I respect your convictions in the matter. Can't you do the same for me? I'm only asking that you be reasonable and kind about permitting me to spend one hour a week in church. Do you love me and respect me that much?"

The late ogre grinned broadly.

There have been no more arguments about her attendance in church on Sunday. Once in awhile he asks her to go with him on Sunday to "make a day of it" in the country. Her Christian life is not dependent upon her attendance at church, it is dependent upon Jesus Christ. And now and then she goes with him for the whole day. She is not doing it in the attitude of mingled guilt and oppression, she is doing it with a fervent prayer in her heart that her going with him *cheerfully* will help open his heart!

A few months after he stopped grumbling about her attendance at church on Sundays, she felt it was the time to bring up the Sunday school question. Their child was two. The mother wanted the boy to go, of course.

She approached her husband in just the same way as before. She reminded him again of his fair-mindedness in his business and social life. She was sitting beside him on the sofa and he had his arm around her as they talked. (Nagging self-righteously from the kitchen never won any argument with any man!)

"I've been thinking a lot about what you said about your

reasons for not wanting Bobby to go to Sunday school. I can see your reasoning. I really can. You want him to be left free to make his own decisions when he is old enough. You don't want him prejudiced by a bunch of Sunday school teachers during his formative years."

Mr. Husband sensed religion coming and he instinctively took his arm from around her shoulders. As though he hadn't, his wife continued quietly.

"There's one thing that puzzles me, though. When he is not being exposed to God, he is being exposed to a life without God. When Bobby is *not* learning how Jesus Christ can help us live creative lives, he *is* learning how to run his life himself! What I don't quite understand in your reasoning is that if you were giving me a valid argument, you would be equally against his starting to school or even playing with his friends. If he must be kept away from church in order to keep an open mind for later on, how are we going to keep him away from the daily things any child does? If he is to have what you call an open mind, he must be protected from everything! Even from Santa Claus and the Easter Bunny."

Her husband lighted a cigarette.

But he didn't have an answer. She waited for several minutes. He got up, threw the match into the fireplace and then sat down again beside her.

He was smoking thoughtfully. Very thoughtfully. This wise little woman was counting on God for every second of this conversation. And she was counting on the love and understanding she really felt in her heart for her husband.

In a few more minutes she spoke again, even more quietly than before.

"It seems to me that what you are saying is that he should have an empty mind. Not an open mind."

Another long moment. "Yeah," he said. "Yeah, it does

work out that way, doesn't it?" That's all he said, but he slipped his arm around her again.

"If Bobby's anything like his father or his mother," she laughed, "he'll still have a mind of his own. I just think he should be exposed to the things of God as well as to fishing and boating and all the other wonderful things you share with him already."

He smashed out his cigarette. "Yeah, never thought about it that way. You may be right. I'm going to line him up for a swimming course at the Y, too, just as soon as he's old enough."

God had won His point. There was no sign or feeling in this wise woman that *she* had won! She was controlled by Christ at the center of her being. He had won and her heart sang.

The boy is six now and in a recent letter she told me that her husband had asked to go to the Children's Day Sunday morning church service to hear his son sing about Jesus Christ. Knowing this woman's open mind and heart toward Christ, and knowing Christ, I expect any day to hear that her husband knows Him, too.

Once again, I remind you that the golden key God used to unlock our sin-hardened and sin-terrified human hearts was the golden key of *identification*. He could have sat on His Throne and mused: "Well, after all I've done for them, with all the intelligence and common sense I gave them, they should be able to do a better job of being my creations. I'll just keep nagging at them through the prophets and sit here until they come to their senses and begin to obey me."

Even as I write these lines, my heart almost bursts with gratitude that He didn't do that!

He identified with us.

He came down here and became *one of us.* He allowed

Himself to experience our fears and heartaches and suffering. As Jesus Christ, He walked the same earth we walk, and was.tempted in His own humanity as we are tempted in ours. And then He stretched out His arms to all of us and let us nail Him to a Cross. God did this because He knew nothing else would work with stubborn humanity!

Wives can do it with their husbands, too. Anyone can identify with anyone else, if she is guided in every step of this identification by the One who used the golden key first.

Ask God to show you, in the particular problem you face with your husband, how to identify with him. Ask Him to show you how it feels to be your husband, with his problems and his needs and his background. Get in it with him. God will be giving you His attention and His sensitivity every minute. His stakes in your husband's life are great. He died for him.

9

The Difference Christ Makes . . .

IN YOUR HOME

9

The Difference Christ Makes . . .
IN YOUR HOME

If Christ stands in the center of your home, it is a happy home.
I did not say if you are a Christian, you automatically
have a happy home. Many Christians are not Christ-controlled at the center of their personalities. And one Christian
in the family is not enough to make a happy home. We are
not being realistic when we say that there are no happy
non-Christian homes. There are. The cause of Christ does
not need rigid concepts to support it. It merely needs Jesus
Christ and willing humanity. Most homes are not happy,
but any home can be, provided Christianity is actively and
consistently practiced in the home. When parents and children are willing to unite around Jesus Christ, then there is
harmony. But there is every appearance of harmony in
many non-Christian homes in which I have been, simply
because the members of the family were united in wanting
to make a happy home.

Most people, however, are too selfish by nature to be
willing to make adjustments merely for the sake of home
unity. This is where the truly Christian home is *realistic*. The
members of that home are not taking a chance on their own
possible unselfishness or merely their desire to be a part of

a "model family." The truly Christian home does not have to depend on unstable human nature. So that the only really safe way to a happy home is through devotion to the one Person who is attractive enough to draw us all out of our selfish ways. This, of course, is God Himself. The Christian home does not *have* to risk the good intentions of mere human nature.

If your home was begun on a Christian basis, you are indeed fortunate. If family devotions have always been a part of your home life, if your children are just as familiar with Jesus Christ as they are with their parents, then you are more than fortunate. You are rare.

But I am thinking right now of one of the truly happy homes about which I know. This is the home of the Gordon Jaeck's in Wheaton, Illinois. They are close, personal friends of mine. Theirs is not only one of the most tastefully decorated and attractive small homes I have ever seen, it is one of the most peaceful. There are two live wire children, the boy, David, about twelve, and the girl, a young teenager, Julianna. They are not goody-goody youngsters. They are natural, attractive, sociable human beings who act their age. And not long ago, Dorothea Jaeck, their mother, told me that she and Gordon were not vital Christians all their lives. In fact, the loss of a baby nine years ago brought them into an awareness of their need. So David and Julianna have not always lived in a vitally Christian home. And the creative atmosphere in which these charming, altogether attractive people named Jaeck live their daily lives, is a fairly recent thing. And simply discounts the oft-quoted theory that it is impossible to change an entire set of family habits once they have been established.

A thoroughly Christian home can be established at any time the parents are united in humbling themselves before the Lord and seeking His guidance in everything.

I am quite aware that there are women reading these pages who envy Dorothea Jaeck because her husband, Gordon, turned to Christ with her. I know that many women are attempting to establish a Christian atmosphere in their home against opposition from all sides. And yet, I feel it is imperative that we as women examine the facts. If one person is really living Jesus Christ in a family, changes can come. I didn't say, "If one person is attending church regularly and sticking up stubbornly for her beliefs." It all hinges on whether or not you, as a woman, are willing to *live Jesus Christ* in your home.

Perhaps right here a brief mention should be made of the necessity for an attractively decorated home. This does not mean expensively decorated. And your taste may be quite different from mine. Here again, no virtue is involved either way. But if you are a messy housekeeper and content with throwing any old colors together, there is deep confusion somewhere in your make-up. And Jesus Christ is *not* "the author of confusion." It so happens that Dorothea Jaeck's taste and mine are similar. Hers is one of the few homes I have ever seen in which I wouldn't want to change something somewhere! And I admit that for a long time after I became a Christian, because my own mother is a "born" decorator, I judged unkindly the homes which didn't appeal to me aesthetically.

Now, I have seen more deeply and my own *prejudices* in decoration (rooted from childhood) have been adjusted by Christ, along with my political prejudices. I wouldn't want an antimacassar on a chair in my living room, but if you like them, I'm only interested in seeing that your antimacassars are clean and well pinned in place!

The feeling of peace in Dorothea Jaeck's beautifully decorated home is not only because of her flawless color sense. It is because Jesus Christ Himself is in control of her, of her husband and of her children. I have spent the night in farmhouses and little prefabricated suburban homes where too many mottoes clashed with too many roses on the walls to which they had been lovingly nailed. But I have felt the same peace and order and security which I feel in the Jaeck home.

I do believe that women should take advantage of the excellent decorating ideas available in any woman's magazine, but it isn't a woman's taste that makes a home peaceful and creative. *It is the woman herself.*

Not long ago I spoke at a women's retreat on the west coast. As a favor to me I asked the women to write down anything they might think would make a helpful addition to this book. One young mother went right to the point and delighted my heart in the process! This is what she wrote: "Before I came to this retreat, I prayed that I would go back to my home to be a better church member, a better women's society member, a better mother, a better wife, a better homemaker. Now, I thank God that He has taken these silly marginal ambitions away! Now I see that all these will come as a result of *knowing Christ,* as He really is."

Another woman wrote: "Jesus, with His outstretched arms has revealed to me in this retreat that He wants my attention all day long. I've been a rude hostess to the Lord in my own home! Greeting Him in the morning and again at night. From now on I will talk to Him all day long about everything. I seem sure for the first time that I do have His attention all day long, and it has made me want to give Him mine. From now on He will be the shining ingredient in my home."

Another wrote: "I want my home to be natural with the naturalness of Christ Himself. I have faced the fact that I am the key to peace in my own home. Without Him I'm not a peaceful person. But with Him I can know peace even during the irritating times."

Still another wrote: "He has shown me during the days of

this retreat that Jesus Christ has really experienced all my temptations and does love me in my every mood and circumstance. I have turned my neurotic, self-pitying emotions over to Him to take care of so I won't carry them at home any more."

These women were facing facts. The fact of their own inadequacy and the fact of Christ Himself. The fact of the great potential in their individual homes if their own personalities are under His loving control.

They were beginning to see that their own lives were setting the rhythm of their homes. If mother is hectic and harried, so is the home. If mother is a messy housekeeper, so will the son and daughter be messy in their dormitory rooms at college. My associate, Rosalind Rinker, noticed this invariably, during the twelve years in which she worked with college students through Inter-Varsity Christian Fellowship. When she visited a student's home, she usually understood the condition of her dormitory room!

In every chapter of this book, we must remember constantly the content of chapter 1. No one's influence is stronger than a woman's influence under any circumstance.

If mother is too busy (even with church work) to pay loving attention to the small but "fabulously important" world of her teen-age daughter, then daughter will be too busy for God.

At a retreat the week following the one in which the women cooperated so lovingly with me on this book, I had an opportunity with girls the age of their daughters! I went directly to a college women's retreat at a Christian college. Here, one girl wrote: "My mother is so busy with civic and church service that she doesn't have time for her own family, and for this reason her love lacks understanding and identification."

I believe no comment is required here. The girl said it all.

Much, much is being written about an avidly sought for

state called "togetherness." It is an admirable ambition. Not only for the home, but for the nation and the world. But to me "togetherness" is merely the description of an idealistic final result of something far deeper.

It would have done no good whatever for God to have remained on His throne and instructed us to "get together" down here in love. We just don't have the ability. Real love which melts away all human personality and prejudice barriers comes only from God. And it is available to us under all circumstances only when Jesus Christ has come to live His life in us. He brings His love with Him when He comes. We have it to use any time we choose to use it. And humanly speaking, even mothers, whose love capacity is so great, will stand up and argue angrily with their families as hot, futile flames of wounded pride and human ego leap from them to scar the lives of those whom they love so much.

Without making direct use of this divine love, women who have been prejudiced in their own youth by background and upbringing are not willing to welcome to their homes, in the Name of Jesus Christ, those who "are beneath them" socially. The doors of a Christian home must be kept open! I do not mean to infer that we become spineless, ridiculous "spiritual socialites." Too many Christians waste precious physical and emotional energy in the name of "sweet fellowship." And once this social ball starts rolling, it is as hard to stop as any other. One night a week, at least, should be legislated for family night. Another for husband and wife to be alone together.

But if someone in need, no matter what his race or state of sobriety or reputation, knocks on the door or rings the telephone on those nights or any other, the doors should *not* be closed.

One of my biggest problems is making my Christian friends understand that during the precious few weeks out of the

year in which I am at home writing on a new book, I can't
fill my evenings with "sweet fellowship." I'd like to. But I
just can't and stay fresh for the next day's work. Everyone
needs some time absolutely alone. Our big tendency is to
grab a quick look at the date book, and if it happens to have
one blank space in the week, to fill it up. We must learn to
say "no," *except* when there is real need. Realizing His un-
changing love for me keeps me from turning down anyone
who is truly needy. The Holy Spirit will define the difference
for us, between real need and someone wanting to be pam-
pered. We can depend upon Him for this. But on the whole,
our homes and our hearts must be kept open.

I know a Christian businessman who led a Negro porter
to the Lord on a train. But he called me to help him find
some Christian homes where the porter would be welcome.
This man's wife wouldn't invite him to her house! (And the
good woman was a great tither and a great tract passer,
too.)

Are you one of those who are still innocently in the dark
on playing God with the new believer or non-believer who
happens to be still smoking? Do you have an ash tray con-
veniently located, even though no one in your family smokes?
Or do you take foolish pride in the fact that there isn't an
ash tray in your house? Think it through. If a man or woman
doesn't mind smoking before God, who are you to say he or
she can't smoke before you? This isn't witnessing. It is refusing to believe that the person who offends you doesn't
need a better knowledge of God in order to change. It is saying he or she should quit because you think so. It is minimiz-
ing the Cross of Jesus Christ, and the Lord Himself had a lot
to say about Pharisaism.

I know another "righteous" soul who is forever trying to
"work with" alcoholics. Things never seem to work out right,
however, because she stands guard over her front door and

refuses to let them come in to talk if they have a bottle in their pocket. She makes them leave it on the front porch or pour it down the sink. If this person hasn't had his old patterns broken by the Holy Spirit yet, this dear soul certainly isn't going to break them by breaking the bottle. She is just wasting money. Because most likely he will go right out her front door and buy another bottle.

"Togetherness" must not stop with members of the family. It must include all who come to your home. No matter who they are or what they are like. And humanly speaking, this is not possible. From a human standpoint some of us will always cringe at certain things. God never cringes. Not even at our pitiable, blind self-righteousness. And if there is to be "togetherness" in your home, there must first be *identification*.

We must do what God did. We must "get in it" with them. I hope no one is fuzzy-minded enough to think I am suggesting that you must take a drink with an alcoholic. But you must, through the power of the Holy Spirit, so identify yourself with that person that you will no longer expect him to be like you overnight! This way your heart will *involve* his heart. As God's heart *involved* your heart on Calvary. This way, your appeal to the person in God's behalf will be seasoned with love, not only with cold doctrine, even if it includes verse and chapter.

God did *not* stay on His remote throne. He came down and became "like unto his brethren." He identified.

This women must do with all guests in their home. This women must do with the members of their families. This is the Spirit of Christ. If He controls your life, identification will become a part of your personality because it is so much a part of His.

10

The Difference Christ Makes . . .

IN THE LIVES OF YOUR

CHILDREN

10

The Difference Christ Makes . . .

IN THE LIVES OF YOUR CHILDREN

"My mom is wonderful in most respects. I just wish she would speak up or at least talk to me about her ideas on sex education. She leaves me out on a limb here. I want to do the right thing, but she acts like it is a dark problem which should be kept in the dark!"

"My mother sent my sister, brother and me to church and Sunday school, but seldom went herself. If she didn't believe in it enough to go, why did she send us?"

"My mother 'loves' me so much, she considers her ideas about my affairs to be correct and never mine. Perhaps this shouldn't be a complaint, but I wish she'd at least give me a chance to think with her! She is sometimes so domineering about it, she makes me feel like a stranger. Or a criminal."

"I wish my mother had more will power: (1) To stand up for the good she knows, but doesn't always show to others. (2) To make her children mind when they are wrong, instead of stopping after just reprimanding us. I'm never quite sure of what she really believes."

"My mother lacks the ability to express affection."

"The thing I long for most is for my mother to be a Christian in thought and deed and not just in words."

"My mother no longer cares about herself or how she looks."

"My mother lacks self-confidence."

"My mother can't talk easily to me, nor I to her."

"I long to be able to talk to my mother about everything. I'm not really trying to hide things. But suddenly a wall goes up between us."

"My mother is always comparing me with someone else—and I come out on the short end! I want her to love me for myself."

"My mother always has to be proven right."

"She doesn't have time for me."

"Mother is always suspecting me of doing some horrible thing. Actually, she puts ideas in my head!"

These are direct quotations from high school and college students, both fellows and girls. As a favor to me, they wrote down on slips of paper their ideas of what is wrong with mothers. Now, before all mothers reading this book crawl shamefacedly beneath the living room carpet or fly into womanly rages, let me say that several young people wrote: "There is nothing wrong with my mother." Or "My mother is just about perfect."

But after looking at some of the honest complaints of young people, realizing that they all came from Christian homes, I believe some honest self-examination is in order.

I have not quoted all the remarks by far. I merely singled out the most representative ones and they all show a few things glaringly:

(1) It *is* a matter of health or sickness to a child's personality whether or not mother's personality is Christ-controlled.

(2) Children want their mothers to have strong identities.

But they also want identities of their own. The girl who said she wished her mother would follow through on her discipline was not alone in this desire. Several others wrote the same thing. Young people don't always see it so clearly, but one of the ways in which parents show love is by discipline. The child wants to feel that the parent is interested enough to follow through. Firm, wise, kindly discipline means that a child is really loved. With the kind of love that cares about the child's personality development.

(3) Young people care terribly about the appearance of their mother.

(4) They long to be confidential with her.

(5) They want her to be sure of her own thinking.

(6) They want her to express her affection.

I discovered nothing new from these youngsters. But I felt it would be helpful to quote them. I am convinced that the frightening *fact* of a mother's ability to mark the lives of her children can never be over expressed. So much has been written about it that some women have confessed they feel like criminals! Others confess boredom. Others resentment at being so important.

But there is great, good hope. Because if a woman is able to damage her child's personality, she is equally able to mark it creatively. The very fact of a mother's influence on her children is, in itself, a neutral thing. It is neither good nor bad. We must keep this in mind. It is the *kind* of marks she makes on her child's life that matter. She is equally as capable of marking beautifully as she is capable of making ugly scars.

This is simply because she is a woman.

And a mother.

After all (although this may be a great blow to mother's ego), a newborn baby does not love its mother at all. It merely has the capacity to learn to love. And it is mother who first loves the child into loving her! Many women adore babies, but resent the reaction of their own personalities on these little darlings as they grow up. As long as an infant is tiny and helpless, mother usually has a fairly easy time of it emotionally. Her own personality, whatever it is, dominates of necessity. The baby hasn't developed one yet.

And the very fact that a mother literally smiles the baby into smiling back at her that first glorious time, sets her lifelong responsibility to that child.

She started this love business!

It is up to her to accept her responsibility all through the years in which the child is with her. Even when he or she is acting like an outsized little hellion.

Especially then.

The newborn child does not love its mother. She loves the baby into loving and depending upon her, by caring for it. It is she who instigates the child's need for her love. It is she who starts the child's dependence upon her.

It is mother who begins it all.

Therefore, it is mother who must continue it through the strange but normal changes which come in the child's personality development.

One woman wrote: "I am absolutely at sea over my teenaged daughter! She has become so remote and peculiar, I feel she is a stranger. I know you don't have children of your own, but I also know you have talked with hundreds of teenagers and I plead with you to give me a hand up! Do you have any clues which might help me understand my daughter? Is she so different? Have I failed so completely? Or is it normal for a girl in her middle teens to 'go away' from the whole family as my daughter has done? She sits bodily at the table with us at dinner, but as quickly as possible, she finds an excuse not to help me with the dishes and dashes off dramatically to her room, sighing heavily and appearing as remote and other-worldly as possible! She spends most of her time in her own room. I understand that she is going through 'that time.' But is my daughter more extreme than most?" No.

She is normal. Apparently this heavy-lidded, highly dramatic, Sarah Bernhardt period varies greatly among teen-aged girls. But it usually comes. In fact, I recently read an excellent article on this subject entitled "She Will Come Back." And she will.

We older people, in quiet desperation, try to keep our humors at this time. And we should. But we should also remember that we, too, "went away" during our teens. Here again, the golden key to unlocking your child's personality and to keeping his or her heart unlocked, is *identification*. It is a noble sounding goal to say there must be "togetherness" between mother and daughter and mother and son. And there must be. But once again, real "togetherness" is the result of *identification*.

Depending upon their rate of personality development and also upon their physical development, teen-aged girls do "go away" from their family circle for a period. And I believe it is right here that most women lose their friendships with their daughters. And with their sons. Because boys have a difficult period of adjustment during these years, too. And no amount of badgering or shaming or scolding or ridicule can bring them back to normal. They are already being normal.

After all, there comes the inevitable time in every teenager's life when the transition just has to be made from childhood to adulthood. It is a tense time for them. A somewhat frightening time in many ways. They pull back toward the dependence of childhood and at the same time they pull toward the brand new world ahead, still to be discovered. Perhaps the pull back toward childhood causes them to appear sullen at times and to resent their parents. For all of their lives up to now, it has been the thing to do to run to mother when things go wrong. Now, suddenly, with the new pull toward maturity, they are embarrassed about doing this. And yet the safety and security of being able to do it still lingers to haunt them. It is involved with mother mainly and so often, they become cross and irritable toward her. And *they* don't understand why.

But teenagers are tender. They have not learned compassion yet, but they have all the tenderness of heart to learn it. They can be reached through their hearts. And usually, at this period, they are more easily reached by *silent* understanding on your part. Don't call attention to the fact that suddenly they're behaving in a peculiar way. They're not. They're just being themselves for their age.

What a deadly thing it is for us to expect young people to act as though they are middle-aged. (Of course, it is equally as deadly for them to expect us to act as though we are young! But more about their side of it in a moment.)

It seems the hardest thing for most mothers to accept the fact that they can only actually *mould* their children's lives to the age of about ten or eleven. From then on, the most that can be done is to *influence* them. The normal psychological state for a child under ten is utter *dependence*. The child depends upon its parents for everything. And this is normal. But parents somehow fail to realize that when the child becomes a teenager, its normal psychological state changes.

The normal state for a teenager is *independence*.

He or she wants to begin to discover life personally. Your daughter wants to think for herself. Your son wants to think for himself. It is here that real friendship between parents and children is *essential*.

And if, as we saw in some of the actual quotations from young people earlier in this chapter, you, as their mothers have not established an easy, natural rapport with them, they will only travel farther away into their own worlds. They still desperately need guidance. But they have begun to think for themselves and they notice and react to the defects in mother's personality. Mother has suddenly become a human being who just could be wrong now and then. They spot your selfishness, your weakness, and although they may let you have it with both barrels in conversation, inwardly they are crushed by what they see. Above all, they want you to be terrific!

Nothing is so important as the way you look and the way you act and your ability to converse, when you visit the campus on mothers' weekend at college. Nothing is so important as the impression you make before the other students and the faculty when you, on some special occasion, visit the high school which is your teenager's world all day long, five days a week.

In all fairness to the young people, I don't think you want the best from them one bit more than they long for the best from you.

But it seems difficult for parents to realize that their children are no longer babies. I admit the transition is fast. Overnight, they seem to be grown up. Grown up and caring about things they never noticed before.

One charming, wholesome, quite intelligent college freshman said to me not long ago: "I know my mother doesn't have the money to dress expensively. She's putting me through college herself. But I wish she had more calmness and peace about her! She is a Christian, but she is always so nervous and ill at ease."

And to prove to you that this fine young lady was not merely complaining, she added: "Genie, how can I help my mother? She has done so much for me. How can I help convince her that it isn't necessary for mothers to be jittery and nervous and unpeaceful if they belong to Jesus Christ? She believes all the right things about Him, but she just doesn't act like it. Every time I go out on a date, she fidgets until I get back. And when I introduce her to any of my friends, she never knows what to say. I'm actually sorry for her, and I wish I could do something to help!"

Teenagers are adults in more ways than we give them credit for being. They are perceptive and sensitive, and down in their hearts they want to become successful adults.

In a note from another young college girl came a striking argument for a Christ-controlled personality if God has given you the responsibility of motherhood:

"The biggest lack in my mother is her inability to show forth Christian love. She would do anything for me or any member of our family. But she is jealous of my friends and criticizes them constantly. She seems to suspect everyone. I know she must love me, but I can't feel a closeness to her and I can't show her affection or confide in her because she doesn't show love to other people, outside of our family! If she would just let herself go and let God's love show through her, I know that together we could win a lot of my non-Christian friends. She shows love to us at home, but not to outsiders. She seems always to be afraid that I'm going to show her up somehow. That she is going to be proven wrong. If she would only just relax and let us love the real woman in her."

From this mother's standpoint, there may be many valid reasons why her personality has become so warped. One of the easiest traps for a mother to fall into is that of over-caring for her family to the exclusion of outsiders. To take care of your family is, in itself, a good thing. But it falls far short of God's love, because it can become quite quickly an *exclusive* kind of love. A love that excludes all for whom you feel no special attraction. All who don't in some way add to the image you have built up through the years of yourself as a splendid, loving homemaker for the members of *your* family.

This young woman longs to love the "real woman" in her own mother. She longs for her mother to be her best self. And the girl sees clearly that the only way this can happen at such a late date (or any date) with her mother is for the woman to allow the love of God to flow through her. His love, remember, is not *exclusive*. It is all *inclusive*.

Evidently this poor woman's mother-love has turned to "smother love." And her daughter is not one bit fooled. In many ways, her daughter is more mature than she.

So far, we have spoken mainly of the failures of mothers. But I am sure that many of you who read this book will be in the position of the teenagers whom I have quoted.

What is your responsibility as daughters?

The same as your mothers'. The glorious, golden key of *identification* which Christ used to unlock all our hearts is yours to use also. And you must learn to use it.

The teen years have been called many things. But certainly, for most of you, they are the years of preparation for motherhood. I am fond of telling teenagers that unless they learn *now* the minute by minute use of the golden key of identification, they will be as troublesome to their children as their parents are to them!

This is true.

Some of us never marry. Most people, it seems, do. And so, most likely, you will. Ask God to show you now, while it is still easy to learn, that He needs your cooperation in the use of this golden key of identification. You may say, "But it's easier for my mother to identify with me. After all, she was my age once. I've never been her age!"

True. But you are reckoning without the availability of the Holy Spirit in your life. He is the Master Identifier. He is One with the Father and with Jesus Christ. And if you ask

Him and stay open to His promptings, He will give you His love and concern and understanding of your mother.

In her excellent book for young people, *The Years That Count* (Zondervan), my associate, Rosalind Rinker, tells the story of one college girl who finally took things in her own hands with her somewhat reserved mother. She prayed about it first with two or three of her Christian college friends, then went home for a weekend, *believing* that God would make an opening for her to ask her own mother to pray with her for the first time.

He did.

And a new, close, warm relationship came into being between that mother and daughter which had existed before on only a rather polite basis of family loyalty.

Mothers are people. Just like you. And if you humble yourself before God first and ask His help in making the right opening, your mother can be approached and God will melt down the barriers. If it doesn't happen the first time, try again. Always believing that He is preparing her heart as well as yours.

Some of you who read this will have sons or daughters in real trouble. My heart goes out to you. So does the heart of God. Perhaps your son or daughter simply will not confide in you. Whether this has been your fault in the past, perhaps only you know. But humbling yourself before your troubled child *can* do no harm. It can only accomplish the purpose of love. God humbled Himself before mankind by coming to the earth as one of us. He asks us to humble ourselves before Him. Love seems only able to flow through humility. So, with your heart bowed before the heart of God, *do* go to your rebellious child and ask him or her to forgive you where you have failed. This may not work at first. But if you persist (not ingratiatingly, but with real humility), you can depend upon the Lord to soften that youngster's heart.

I remember one glorious moment behind a coat rack in the basement of a midwestern church seven years ago. I don't remember the name of the mother and her daughter, but the daughter was pregnant and barely seventeen. Somehow she had agreed to come to the Mother and Daughter Banquet where I was speaking. Both were in tears. Both wanted the confidence of the other.

"There has always been a horrible barrier between Mother and me," the girl sobbed. "How do we get rid of it? I need her now if I ever needed her."

I answered, "We'll ask God to melt the barrier down."

"Somewhere along the line I've lost touch with my daughter," the mother wept. "We've tried to talk about this terrible thing that's happened, but we always end up arguing. How can we get rid of this wall between us?"

I answered, "We'll ask God to melt it away."

With one arm around each of them and their arms around each other, we did just that. And He melted it away.

I did nothing but *identify* with them both. Perhaps you and your daughter need an understanding outsider to do this with you. But perhaps your daughter won't agree to this until you've humbled yourself and asked her help in it, too.

That outsider could be your minister. It could be a friend. Or a chance acquaintance, as I was with that mother and her daughter seven years ago. God will guide you if you ask Him to do it. But if your own ego and hurt pride stand in the way, simply because your daughter is not, at the moment, a huge success, little will be accomplished. She is still your daughter. You are still her mother. She needs you now more than she has ever needed you. If you appear shocked and angry (no matter what she's done!) you are acting totally unChristian. "While we were yet sinners, Christ died for us," showing no shock or anger at our being as we are.

If He is controlling your personality, you will be enabled

to show the same kind of quiet love. You have full access to His love, because you have full access to Him.

Perhaps the greatest and kindest thing you could do for your children is to love them into loving Jesus Christ. They are difficult only as *their* personalities are not under His control. If you have become a Christian late in life, your problem is greater. But your love, which has the enviable and responsible place of having put its roots down into your child's heart *first,* in babyhood, can be the instrument which Christ uses to reach that heart.

If you have been a "preachy" mother and railed at your children for not attending church, then this is a different matter. My grandmother did this to me when I was a child, and I made a break from all of it the minute I went away to college! Jesus Christ did not come to condemn or to rail, He came to save. His "longsuffering is our salvation." And He can change you.

Many of you who read this will be genuine Christian women who want to be good mothers. Your children are also Christian.

I remember as I write, one attractive woman about my age, who talked to me in a bookstore one day.

"Genie, the kids aren't afraid to speak up to you. What do they think is wrong with their mothers? I want to know if and where I am failing my daughter. She is in her early teens and before trouble comes, I want to be set right. How far should I go in telling her what she can and cannot do? How far can I go, how far must I go and yet not turn her against Christ in the process?"

This woman's honesty was one of the first seeds the Lord planted in my mind which prompted the writing of this book. That was two years ago at Mt. Hermon, California. That very day, when I spoke to the high schoolers at the same conference, I began collecting answers to the question I have since asked over hundreds of miles of hundreds of teen-agers: What is wrong with your mother? Some of these an-swers you have found in this book.

As to how far you as a mother should go in insisting that your child *not* do this or that, I believe only the Holy Spirit can tell you exactly. Because only He knows your child and only He knows the circumstances of his or her life, and only He knows how vital is the child's own faith in Jesus Christ. All of these things are relevant. We do not live under reli-gious legalism. I know that many well-meaning Christian par-ents will refuse to allow their children to attend selected movies and at the same time continually expose these chil-dren to gossip and irritability and jealousy and Class B movies on the television set at home. I am not recommending that you allow your child to see selected movies and I am not recommending that you do not. But I *am* urging you from my heart to let that child see Jesus Christ in control of your per-sonality!

The Bible does not say that we become Christian or re-main Christian because we do not do this or that. But it does say, "Believe on the Lord Jesus Christ and thou shalt be saved."

Believing on Him means that we depend upon Him not only for our salvation, but for our dispositions and our wis-dom. If you really believe on Him, you can depend upon His giving you personal guidance about each of your children.

The more I see sincere Christians crowded behind their man-made walls of do's and don'ts, the more I understand why it is that so few outside those walls ever discover Christ. I am not suggesting compromise of any sort. I am suggesting that we need to begin to look squarely at the *one* central is-sue: Jesus Christ Himself.

I have dedicated this book to my own mother because I love her. But I have also done it because she and I have seen the theme of this book proven in our own relationship. We were always close. But now that both our personalities are invaded by the Spirit of Christ, we are not only closer than ever before, we have each found a new respect for our own personalities in relation to each other.

Jesus Christ can only mark a child's personality in a completely creative way. If He is in control of a mother's personality, her marks upon her child's life will be creative, too.

Mothers *can* be what the greeting card versifiers claim that they are, if they belong to Jesus Christ at the very center of their beings.

It may seem too late under your particular circumstance. Let me assure you it is never too late if He is on the scene.

11

The Difference Christ Makes . . .

IN YOUR UNMARRIED LIFE

11

The Difference Christ Makes . . .

IN YOUR UNMARRIED LIFE

Many of you who read this book will be, like myself, unmarried women. It has ceased to matter to me whether the rest of the world calls us spinsters, old maids, bachelor women or career women.

It has ceased to matter to me, actually, when someone waxes inquisitive enough to ask why I'm not married! Oddly enough, no one ever asked this question until I became a Christian. I moved about in a world where many women were married to their careers and no one seemed even interested in the fact that I had never married a man. Christians, however, are rather nosey on this point, and since there is seemingly no satisfactory explanation in my case, I was somewhat at a loss as to what to say for the first few years of my Christian life. Now that I know the Lord Jesus better, I just smile and let it go. Occasionally I quote the handsome lady missionary whose answer I still find most accurate. Toward the end of her life, someone asked her to comment on her spinsterhood. She is said to have smiled charmingly and answered: "Well, being married is *one* circumstance of the Christian life and being single is *another* circumstance of the Christian life."

In other words, if Christ Himself is in the center of our lives, either circumstance is workable. And either circumstance is desirable. I believe she inferred, too, that either circumstance can be undesirable!

I happen to be single by choice, but if this is any comfort to those of you who are *not*, most of my problem mail comes from married women. I believe theirs *is* the most difficult role. But while I have never been willing to face the complications of married life myself, I do not for one minute discount the ache which may be in your heart for a husband and children of your own.

Some of you who read this will be women whose hearts have been broken by the unfaithfulness of a man. Many of you will be widows. Others will have tasted and retasted the gall of loneliness because the one to whom you were to have been married died before the marriage took place. Others will have choked on the still greater bitterness of having him change his mind about loving you at all.

Some of you have just never been asked.

This may be the bitterest blow of all to any woman. I rather imagine it is.

Still others among you may have lost the chance to marry because you have had the care of an invalid parent. This can cause deep hostility. Others, if Christ is on the scene, have made good lives for themselves and for the parents. But this is an unnatural situation and even though the bitterness may have been kept away by the Presence of Christ, the ache and the frustration may always be with you.

I learned recently that thirty-nine per cent of the missionaries on foreign fields are men. The rest are, in the main, single women. There is no doubt but that the Lord calls some women to Himself. If He needs a woman's touch to fulfill a certain portion of His work, there are times when He cannot share her with a husband and a family.

In my own work, I fail to see how there would be time for me to be a homemaker. Being a good wife and mother and homemaker is a career in itself. I do not mean to infer that mothers who work cannot be good mothers. But certainly it is not the ideal way.

In fact, I would like to make it clear here that God does not seem to deal in ideals at all. He works with *reality*. If we are centered in Him, He will make creative use of whatever circumstance surrounds our lives.

And with this in mind, I would like to share with you some of what I have learned about Christ's answer to the frustrations in the lives of unmarried women.

For the first part of this chapter, we will speak of those who have never been married and of divorcees.

In the remainder of the chapter, we will be speaking of widows.

Be sure that Jesus Christ is equally concerned about all of you.

Single Women

"I don't know why I'm pouring all this out to you, except that you are single, too, and I thought perhaps you'd understand."

I receive many letters which begin this way. Here is one I would like to share with you.

"I've been a Christian since I was a child. I shared the jitters of my single girl friends when the years went by and I found myself still unmarried. I had some dates. But somehow nothing ever came of any of them. My home life was miserable and I left home as quickly as I could. Then one by one my single girl friends were no longer single. And one horrible day I woke up to find I was alone. They were all married. I always believed that my questionable home life was the reason for it. I was from the wrong side of the tracks. Not ugly, not pretty. I'm just average. And I honestly tried to build a life for myself. I worked my way through college and have a good job. I am 43 now and still alone. I've lived alone all my life since I left home.

"There doesn't even seem to be a place for me at church. Last Sunday one of the older women said to me, 'We just don't know what to do with you. You're too old for the young people's group and you're too young for us to put you in with the older ladies. If only you were married, we could put you in with the married group.'

"Her words were like acid on my heart. And I have collapsed under it for the first time. The way I feel now I'm never going back to church again. I've tried to live a Christian life. I've always been the first to volunteer to visit the jails and hospitals. I've tried to cooperate and not be an oddball. But an unmarried woman just *is* an odd ball! And I hate it. I resent it with all my heart. Now that I've written this much I realize I probably shouldn't have done it. You couldn't really understand the spot I'm in. You're in the Lord's work and busy all the time. I guess what I want to know from you is do you really think it is a sin to commit suicide?"

This letter was one of the most difficult I've ever had to answer. But I wrote something like this: "Suicide is probably no more of a sin than any other selfish act. But I am no judge of this. And I don't intend to comment further on it, except to say that you did not shock me when you mentioned it. Not one bit. Even though I happen to feel no complaints about my single life, I do understand the ache in your heart at not fitting anywhere in the life of your church. But I beg you for Jesus' sake, to stop long enough to look beyond the social framework of a man-organized church to Christ Himself.

"No one walked a more lonely road than He walked when He was on earth. And those of us who are single can, of all people, really know that He identified with us! He was single, too. It has seemed to me as though He lived His life in many ways so as to be able to identify with the most wretched among us. Surely this is one way. And while I know you feel like an odd ball among the married couples who seem to be able to talk about nothing but their children, you are *not* an odd ball with Jesus. He knows. And while they are chattering away about their families, realize that they are not forced into the blessed position into which life has forced you! You are in many ways fortunate. But you must look beyond the people around you before you will get what I mean. Anyone who is a fringe personality is blessedly forced to depend solely upon Christ. And this is, in the truest sense, a marvelous thing!

"God's *great* apostle, Paul, was apparently unmarried. And when I read his writings, I know I am reading not only God's inspired truth, I am reading the outpourings from the heart of a man who has experienced what he is writing about! It is often hard for single people to take advice from a happily married person. But Paul has a human as well as a divine right to say, 'I would have you without carefulness. He that is unmarried careth for the things that belong to the Lord, how he may please the Lord: but he that is married careth for the things that are of the world, how he may please his wife. There is difference also between a wife and a virgin. The unmarried woman careth for the things of the Lord, that she may be holy both in body and in spirit: but she that is married careth for the things of the world, how she may please her husband. And this I speak for your own profit; not that I may cast a snare upon you, but for that which is comely, and that ye may attend upon the Lord without distraction' (I Corinthians 7:32–35).

"I don't for one minute think that Paul was instructing anyone to avoid marriage if it is in God's will. He carefully mentioned that he said these things *not* to cast a snare upon anyone. I believe this passage is included in God's Word so that should we find ourselves in this position, we can know that great, creative good can come from it."

I ended my letter by telling her I did not think she was facing *spiritual* facts. No matter what life offers or deprives we must make a love-offering to Jesus Christ of our bitterness at life. It is really bitterness at God if we are honest. I urged her to *accept* her lot and then deliberately put on an attitude of expectancy. When Jesus Christ is in charge, we have every right to expect Him to do something creative with our tragedies. I suggested that she offer her services as a Sunday school teacher with younger people. The insensitive, thoughtless sister who reminded her of the predicament in which her spinsterhood had placed them all, was dead wrong in reminding her. But she, with her singular need for Christ, is in a position to receive from Him far more than this woman who feels no need. And the single woman can "turn it to a testimony" by getting them off the hook with some humor on her part. Teaching younger people would also help fill her empty life.

This particular advice concerning the Sunday school class may not apply to your problem. But if in your heart, you are building an explosive resentment against life because you are not married, you, too, must realize that God had a purpose for including in His Word the message Paul wrote in I Corinthians seven.

Up and down the little side street on which I live shuffle lone women. Near derelicts. It is a strange street because up and down its sidewalks pass wealthy women in mink coats and women in tattered coats who stop at every garbage can in the alley beside my house, hunting food and any castoff items they may sell in order to buy a drink. One old woman's name is Edith. I have spoken to her many times during the years in which I have lived here. She hates God. She is usually quite drunk and her cracked old whisky voice literally shrieks at the sky when I mention Him to her. "God? I hate Him! If He's even there, He shouldn't be! He must be a devil to leave an old woman like me alone in the world, grubbin' a livin' out of garbage cans!"

I can only go on loving Edith and praying for her and helping her all I can. Until she sees that God came down here and became one of us in Jesus Christ, she will continue to rail at heaven and curse Him for her own pitiable existence.

If you are alone in the world and don't know Christ, you can know Him. And *only* in knowing Him personally will you find a way to end your loneliness. Bitter, self-pitying people are always alone. Other people can't cope with them.

On my radio program, "Visit With Genie," I interviewed at least five women who live alone under varying circumstances. Women whose lives are under the control of Jesus Christ. All with deep problems to face, but all living creative, generally uncomplaining lives. One woman, Margaret Williams, gave me a striking closing for the program on which I interviewed her. She is a social worker, alone in the world. I invited her to appear on my series just a few weeks after her mother, her last living relative, had died. Margaret is unmarried, in her forties, and lives alone in a rented apartment. But so definitely is Christ in control of her personality that her closing line on the interview was this: "The only real complaint I have, Genie, is that I just don't have enough time alone to read the books I want to read!"

Perhaps you have refused to give up your right to have been married. Perhaps you are saying, "It isn't right that I should be single and all my sisters married with homes of their own." If this is the thought-line in your heart, you are clinging to your rights. You are not accepting life as it is.

And, I repeat, people who cling to the right to themselves are usually lonely.

Many women write to me complaining that they would make it, too, as Christians, if they had someone to live with as I have. I can only say this: God seems to be aware that I need someone to help me if I am to continue to work in the many different fields in which I now work. Should the time come when He could make better use of me alone, I would simply have to be willing to be alone.

God doesn't permit us to operate on *our* understanding of His ways. Many Christ-centered women live alone and will always be alone. Like my friend, Margaret Williams. *But* she has accepted it and is living life to its fullest, regardless. So, don't get any ideas that God will reward you with a roommate, just for giving up your rights. He is free to send someone to you then, and probably He will. But the heart of the matter is that we accept our lives as they are now and leave the future to Him.

What of you if you are a divorcee? Perhaps you have children to support. I interviewed a woman in this predicament on my radio series, too. A close friend of mine whose husband deserted her when her little girl was three. The daughter is a lovely, balanced teenager now. And although life has been anything but easy for my friend, and although she was not a Christian when her husband deserted her, she has taken hold of the great potential of the Christian life and is discovering every day that no one is really alone, *if* she belongs to Jesus Christ. At the time of her conversion this woman was intensely bitter. Now, she is among the best company I know. I don't see her often, but I know when I do, I'll learn something more of the true humor and wisdom of heaven!

Perhaps the deepest scar of all is left on a woman's heart when a man deserts her for someone else. But because of what Jesus Christ is like, this too, can be healed, and He makes all scars radiant. He seems to use them to deepen our characters and enhance our personalities. This woman, whose life would have been so tragic and whose personality so distorted if she had attempted to carry her load without Christ, is one of the most natural and delightful people I know. Even when her beloved daughter, for whom she had worked so hard, was seriously ill not long ago, the center of her life held. And it held because *she was being held* by Christ Himself.

At a big hospital in Michigan City, Indiana, lives another friend of mine. A dear little lady in her late sixties, who pushes the carts of food up and down the corridors of the hospital for a living. Hattie is all alone in the world. She was once an alcoholic.

So far as I know, her only mail is an occasional note from me. She lives alone in a little room at the hospital. She is shy and doesn't make friends easily. But she has one Friend who takes excellent care of her. I'm planning to visit her as soon as I finish this book. For Hattie's sake? No, for mine. She always has a little ribbon in her curly white hair and she always has a lift for me. Life dealt her a dreadful blow thirty-five years ago when the man she loved left her. She was on her way to Lake Michigan to kill herself. By divine chance, she got off the streetcar at a wrong corner. And on that corner was a mission, where Christ was waiting for her. They have been friends ever since. Her secret is that she has stayed grateful.

Another woman, respected in her community, was deserted by her husband. Hers was the great humiliation. They were both prominent in the town. Everyone knew about it. After twenty-five years of married life, he left her for another woman. The days dragged along, and this woman was dragged with them. She knew Christ. But slow, slow is the human heart to respond to His healing touch. This is no fault of ours. It is the way we are. Her heartache never really ended. Her lovely home remained empty. But through the five remaining years in which she lived, she taught me a great many things. He did not promise perpetual happiness. But He did promise that He would be with us through everything. Until He mercifully took her home, He stayed right with her in the empty house. He supplied her frail little body and her troubled heart with His own strength and love, so that she had enough of both to give to youngsters who needed her, to old persons who needed her, to her church where her life glowed in a way it had never glowed before. Through this woman's gentle acceptance of the blow life handed her, "phoniness" dropped away like dead leaves from the lives of many of the women in her church. Her last five, sometimes agony-filled, years were turned to a shining testimony for the value of a Christ-controlled personality.

In every life there is *aloneness*. This is normal. I am sure those of you who read this book in your own homes, surrounded by your own children, perhaps waiting for your husband to come home for dinner, also experience times of feeling absolutely alone. The secret is that we can come to the place of realizing that we are created this way. God has reserved a place for Himself only, down in the very center of our beings. And our trouble springs from the fact that we try to fill this place with other things and other people. It is reserved for Christ himself. Nothing else really fits. And we must not fall into the confusion of mistaking normal *aloneness*, which is intended to draw us to God, with *loneliness!*

Active, Christ-centered Christians are seldom lonely. Women who live alone and who are well adjusted are simply those who have recognized this secret place as His and have allowed Him to enter and take possession. The maladjusted among us experience this *aloneness*, leap to the wrong conclusion, and begin to scream that we are *lonely!*

Loneliness is different from *aloneness.*

It is well for us to check our lives on this point now and then. It may prevent great trouble later on. I find myself aware of the *aloneness* at the center of my being sometimes more acutely when I am on a platform or in a crowd. But I no longer feel isolated from people because of it. I feel driven to Christ, who is always there in that *aloneness*, ready to give me what I need at the moment. For several years after I became a Christian, I felt quite alone among God's people. With many I seemed to have little in common socially. And about this time I read Anne Lindbergh's great little book *Gift from the Sea.* Everyone should read her chapter on *Aloneness.* She doesn't mention Christ, but He mentioned Himself to me as I read the beautiful book one day on a train coming home from a series of meetings during which I had been much aware of my aloneness. I saw that this aloneness is normal. And that it is not loneliness until I mistake it as such! From that moment, I have welcomed the times of being aware of the secret place at the center of my being which no human being can fill. And which I have no right to try to force a mere human being to fill.

This is our big mistake. Mothers try to force their children into this place. Wives their husbands. Friends other friends. It is reserved for God. That is why most of the world is lonely. They do not know that there is One who longs to fill their aloneness with Himself.

Widows

Here are excerpts from several letters which I received from a woman recently widowed.

"I am writing from my end of the breakfast table. Somehow

I never realized before what a long table this is! But the atmosphere is made fragrant with love from all those who have shared love with me here. Most of the time now I am alone, but I am learning that I never have to feel lonely any more. I have gone through many stages since Daddy left to be with the Lord a few weeks ago, but when I need Christ, He is always here. All I need to do is *look at Him!* We can be anything we want to be in the Lord. Or we can be burdens to our loved ones. When my heart sinks with missing Daddy (as it does so often) I look up fast and say out loud, 'Lord, You are such a wonderful Saviour! You have given me so much. Thank You, oh, thank You that my dear one isn't suffering anymore. Thank You that I know he is happy with You and waiting, with You, for me.' Invariably (even when I'm not expecting it) He gives me new courage beyond explanation. It is as though I ask for just one thing and He gives me a dozen! Not only companionship, but love, and courage and hope and such a great desire to show Him to other women who have collapsed because a dear one has gone. We make Him such a weak Lord when we allow our minds to settle on ourselves. The tears still flow, but quickly I have formed the habit of saying, 'Do something creative with me, Lord. These tears will never bless anyone else's life.'

"Is there a word for joy and strength while going through grief? I don't know, but I do know that I am given comfort and a strange inner joy, while the tears flow. It is all very slow. But I am climbing the steps to readjustment with Him. He knows we can't take in all He has for us at once. We must be told a little at a time.

"I was lying in bed one evening, with my books and radio on Daddy's empty bed beside me. Thinking of how my dear one had suffered through those long weeks. God spoke again. 'Your anxiety can be turned into constructive thoughtfulness for the future. Let the past sleep, but let it sleep on My bosom.' That was a real turning point for me. Simple? Yes. But He knew that was what I needed. I had been tormenting myself and wasting good hours paying attention to the way my heart still ached over his suffering before he left me. Remembering the endless blood transfusions, his poor little thin, needle scarred hands (hands which were once so strong and handsome and capable). Still longing to be able to do something to help him just once more. Ministers and Christian friends had tried to tell me how to keep my chin up. And their advice fell flat. But to place my dear one's suffering on the bosom of the Lord like a lovely rose—this was different. I said, 'All right, Lord. I will do that right now.' And I did.

"I miss him so much every hour of the day. Terribly at communion in church last Sunday. My heart is so broken. Yesterday, I had a particularly hard time when I heard a horn like his toot twice (as he always tooted at the top of the driveway). For just a moment, the habit of the years caught me and I thought, 'Oh, he's coming home.' Then I remembered that he would never toot at me again and that he would never come home again. But so definitely, when I turned to the Lord for help, He said, 'Why don't you sing to Me? Things can't be dark when you are singing.' I said, 'All right, Lord, I'll sing.' I remembered I hadn't sung since Daddy left, except in church. So now I have a new habit. I sing my prayers sometimes, making up the tunes as I go. I had forgotten, in all my grief, about the release in singing! He said He would not leave us comfortless. And, by His grace, I am driving a stake right there, as Daddy would have said. Even when I just have to walk the floor to keep from collapsing, I find that His love comes pouring through. All I need to do ever, is to keep my window open to Him. Minute by minute I keep aware that He has said, 'Lo, I am with you alway.'

"I have heard you say and I have read over and over in your book *Share My Pleasant Stones*, that He is a Redeemer *of all things,* if we will but come to Him with them. I know your heart is heavy with grief, too, because you and Daddy were so close. You are so like him. But, although we were separated quickly by your travel schedule after the funeral, I know He will guide my little one as she travels bringing His love to people so hungry for that love."

Perhaps some of you have discovered as you have read these quotations, that they are parts of letters from my own mother, written to me since the recent death of my beloved dad.

If pages permitted, I would like to share many more of these letters with you. But I have shared these few, so that you who are faced with adjusting to a new way of life alone, without the one who was always with you in it, can know that I understand. I haven't experienced widowhood. But I am living through these days in close identification with my own mother, who is experiencing it. Her letters have been an amazing source of strength to me in my own grief over the home-going of my father.

She has not burdened me with her times of agony. But she has shared some of her victory in them with me by letter. They would have heaped unbearable weight upon my already grief-loaded heart, had she failed even once to end the sharing with the glorious lesson Christ had taught her from it. When my father left us, Mother lost not only her best friend, her lover and her playmate, she lost her work, too. My father was a dentist and she was his assistant. They were together twenty-four hours a day. So her adjustment is a minute by minute thing. And because both my brother and I travel almost constantly, she has been alone with Christ in it.

Along with learning to live without him, she must learn how to throw off the times of re-living the long months of his suffering with him. This has been difficult for us all. But Dad gave us a great deal to live up to here. Should Mother, or my brother Joe, or I be called upon to suffer someday as Dad suffered, we have a great example before us. He lived Jesus Christ right up to the last minute of his earthly life, when he died with horrible secondary complications from acute leukemia, his bed soaked with his own blood and the blood of the wonderful Christian friends who kept the transfusion bottles filled and ready.

Life is not beautiful all the time. But through the ugliness and pain and agony and loneliness, there is available to every human being the fragrance of the very Presence of Christ.

And He *is* a Redeemer. Nothing needs to be wasted in His Presence.

My mother is well aware that she is the one who will choose whether or not her grief is to be wasted. She knows that Christ can make glorious, creative use of it, if she allows Him to pour out her life now to others who need her.

No one will ever take Dad's place for her and she has accepted this. One night I shared with her what the Lord had given me in conversation with another widow several years ago. It had come to me to ask this other widow if she were trying to allow Jesus Christ to take the place of her husband. She thought a minute and said, "Yes, I guess I am. And it isn't working." Jesus Christ longs to heal us realistically. He is not a substitute. He is Himself.

My mother, in still another letter, has expressed this more clearly than I can express it: "Yesterday, as your brother Joe and I stood in the cemetery on the hill where dear one's body lies, God was in the wind and although tears flowed, this thought came to me: The things that happen do not happen by chance. They happen entirely in the decree of God. He is working out His purposes. And He has enough love to fill your empty heart and mine. But I have learned that we only realize this when we blot out of our thoughts everyone 'save Jesus only.' He is trying to be Himself with me as I allow Him to do it. He understands my missing Daddy so much. He doesn't shame me or belittle me. He just calls to me to look *at Him* only! And when I do, such comfort floods my whole being that I can only thank Him. Much depends upon our discipline of mind."

Other letters come from other widows. Some are as courageous in the strength of God as my own mother. One woman, because she couldn't afford to buy so many copies of my daily devotional book, *Share My Pleasant Stones*, began typing off certain passages and mailing them to hospitals and institutions where human beings were suffering physically and emotionally in spiritual darkness. Countless persons were brought into a close relationship with Christ. And the widow's own life was filled to overflowing as a result of her lovely "new work." Until she began it, she had spent her days in weeping over photographs of her husband.

Recently another letter came. But this one was from a widow who had pulled down her blinds, and turned to sleeping pills and alcohol to deaden her grief. A neighbor had given her a copy of my life story, *The Burden Is Light*. Her letter was a last plea to know for sure that God did exist!

Surely we can't blame this woman for turning to sleeping tablets and alcohol. She doesn't know Christ.

I am sure the human tendency is to pull down the blinds and try to find an escape from the constant pain of realization that the loved one is never coming back in this life. This is the *natural* thing to do. But we have access to the *supernatural*. Night after night, my mother lies sleeplessly on her bed repeating, "Lord, I know your strength is made perfect in my weakness." And it is. Eventually she sleeps. And gradually she is sleeping a little better. A few minutes longer each night.

Usually only those who have experienced widowhood can

or will take time to understand the slowness with which time heals. But time is one of God's greatest instruments of healing. And it is important for you who are living through this time of adjustment now, to realize that each day brings more relief than you imagine it is bringing. The Lord has commissioned us to "go into all the world." This includes widows. He means for you to go, too. If Christ lives in your mortal body, my prayer is that He will not allow you to be satisfied with pulling down your blinds. He needs you and unless you allow Him to make creative use of your grief, then your husband *and* Christ will have died in vain!

With the widow as with the single woman, God sends companionship and friends, according to how much we have given up the rights to ourselves. If my mother felt sorry for herself because my brother travels so much and has a family of his own to take his time and attention, or if she resented or even secretly resisted my work which keeps me away from her, God's hands (mighty as they are) would be tied in His efforts to fill her life as He longs to fill it.

We can't expect other people, even our closest and dearest friends and relatives, to make our adjustments for us. We must make our own, through Christ.

But I am the first to agree that when life forces us to live alone, real adjustment is a near impossibility if it is inspired by mere good intentions.

More words about the necessity of a Christ-controlled personality in a woman's unmarried life seem extraneous. So there will be no more, except this breathed prayer that you, no matter what your circumstances, if you are alone, will right now give over the controls of your entire life into the hands of Jesus Christ.

He is the only adequate definition of love which I know.

He will turn your tears to living water. Remember, it was

Jesus Himself who said: "Whosoever drinketh of the water that I shall give him shall never thirst; but the water that I shall give him shall be in him a well of water springing up into everlasting life."

12

The Difference Christ Makes . . .

IN YOUR FRIENDSHIPS

12

The Difference Christ Makes...

IN YOUR FRIENDSHIPS

"Mrs. Mary Woodrum, a widow about 55, jumped to her death early this morning from her apartment on the twelfth floor of —— Street on the north side of Chicago. Just before she jumped, she saw the building's janitor working on another window across the thirty foot court. Mrs. Woodrum waved to him. He waved back. And then she jumped to her death. On her orderly writing desk, Mrs. Woodrum left this note: 'I can't stand one more day of this loneliness. No sound from my telephone. No mail in my box. No friends.' On the sixth floor of the same big city apartment building lives Mrs. J. Jenkins, another widow. Mrs. Jenkins told reporters: 'I wish I had known she was so lonely. I could have called on her. We could have been friends.'"

Friendships are as much a part of the "more abundant life" which Jesus came to bring as any of His other great gifts. Without them, life is an empty thing. We need mail in our box. We need telephone calls from our friends. We need friends. We need to know someone cares about us.

When one has lived as long as I have lived in a big city, one learns to spot quickly the lonely people who walk the noisy streets. There is a different look on their faces. No matter how well fed or how well dressed, there is still the look of hunger about them.

They are lonely. They need friends. Just one friend would change their whole outlook on life. Some of them sit in the parks, hoping another human being will sit down beside them on the park bench. They feed the pigeons and the squirrels but their own hungry hearts go unfed. Some of them are ill. Just yesterday, I saw an elderly man out trying to learn to walk again alone. Obviously he had suffered a stroke. He dragged one leg noticeably. He was pale and drawn and unsteady. And he was alone, trying to rebuild his frail body about which no one apparently cared. I helped him across the icy street, but I couldn't understand him when he spoke. The paralysis was not limited to his leg.

Around the corner on LaSalle Street, when I got out of a cab not long ago, I stopped and sat down in a doorway beside an unkempt, toothless, drunken woman of Mexican or Puerto Rican birth. I tried to talk to her. I offered to take her to a corner restaurant. But all she would mumble over and over in her broken English was, "Nobody cares. Nobody cares. Nobody cares." She wouldn't get up from the doorstep. I gave her a piece of paper with the name and address of the Women's Division of the Pacific Garden Mission written on it. I doubt if she went. She couldn't believe I was anything but curious. No one had cared for so long.

Those of us who have been given the light of Christ's Presence have no excuse for being friendless.

If you are a friend, you will have friends.

And surely, if He is in control of your personality you will not only have friends, you will be one. And you will know how to be a creative friend. I am aware that some of you who read this book now may appear friendless. Even if we are centered in Jesus Christ, now and then the circumstances of our lives leave us feeling alone. But I feel quite safe in writing that if you are His, there are persons somewhere who really care about you.

I would be the last to discount the fact that some human personalities are more attractive than others. You may be shy. You may not be an outgoing personality. If this is true, then you find it more difficult to make friends. But the bonds of love in Jesus Christ leap all self-conscious barriers, if pleasing Him is our first purpose. Too many of us are Christian-type people-pleasers. This is not being controlled by Christ. It is being controlled by people and what they think of us.

Some of you may be new Christians and you may feel friendless simply because you still feel strange with other Christians and have dropped some of your pursuits in which you felt so comfortable with your old friends. Believe me, I understand your feeling of aloneness.

You may be reading this book in a hospital or sanatorium where you see your friends from home so seldom that you feel friendless, too. In a sanatorium at Stateville, North Carolina, lies a young girl who is bedfast. But far from friendless. I look forward to Bonnie's mail because her letters are real lifters to me. She hasn't known Jesus Christ for very long, but she is making up for lost time now. Her entire life, body, emotions, mind and spirit are completely under His control and her mail is heavy because she reaches out through it to others; and because she is a friend to those around her in the sanatorium, she is far from lonely.

If He is first with us, we *have* to give of ourselves to other people. This requires no premeditation on our part. We may resist inwardly or even outwardly for a minute, but if He is in control, we end up giving! Because He is the great Giver.

"For God so loved the world that He *gave*. . . ."

And when we give, we receive, provided we have not given *in order* to receive.

Becoming a Christian has made a complete revolution in my own life where people are concerned. Before I was His, I selected my friends. I have not become an automaton, I still have preferences. But I've found that most of my friends now are the ones He has selected for me. I also find that my spiritual life runs smoothly or it bumps along in direct proportion to how much I am submitting to or fighting His choices.

Before we go further with the subject of close friendships, I would like to say something about casual relationships. The butcher, the baker, the grocer, the filling station operator, the clerks in the stores which we patronize. I am convinced that there is no better Christian witness than Christlike behavior at a bargain counter! I am seldom in one place long enough to know about bargains, but the same principle holds true when I stand in a service garage facing the mechanic who promised my car for three P.M. and who now tells me it will be noon tomorrow. It is during these times in our casual relationships when we discover what is really inside us. When we discover who is really at the controls. Belonging to Christ has automatically formed this thought pattern in me: No matter where I am, or with whom I am in contact, that person *could* find out that I'm a follower of Jesus Christ and if I act unlike Him, He will have to take the blow for me!

If He is uppermost in all our thoughts, we do not have to prod ourselves to remember Him. We realize that we have His reputation in our hands wherever we go. No Christian ever stands up to make a suggestion or refute one in a committee meeting without a reflection of some kind on the very Person of Jesus Christ. No Christian has business dealings

with the window-washer or the laundry man without a reflection on Jesus Christ. The committee meeting may be at
P.T.A. or at a Garden Club conclave, but if you are a Christian, His reputation is at stake.

If He is in control of your personality, you will remember
this, and you will act accordingly.

We do not need to be highly trained, full-time Christian
workers to remember Jesus. During the last days of my own
father's life in the hospital, I watched Christ's control of his
personality work over and over again. Both his arms and
hands held so many needle punctures that one day when he
was very, very weak and ill, three doctors had to be called
before one finally managed to set a satisfactory transfusion.
The doctors were highly nervous. But their love and respect
for my dad's Christianity grew because it was he who kept
encouraging them! It was he who kept making jokes with
them and reminding them that they'd make it all right because he had turned it over to the Lord before they came
into his room.

In hospitals, in beauty salons, in grocery stores, in banks,
in garages, in committee meetings, when the doorbell or the
telephone rings, every minute of every day we have the reputation of Jesus Christ to remember. We cannot remember
flawlessly. No one has that kind of memory. But if He is in
control at the center, He will always act and react exactly
like Himself. "Jesus Christ, the same yesterday, today and
forever." Under all circumstances.

We have an excellent barometer to indicate the condition
of our spiritual lives in our casual relationships. But what of
our close friendships? Any Christian who is Christ-controlled
will have some friends. Because if He is in control of you,
then He is the most prominent part of your personality. And
He has said, "I, if I be lifted up . . . will draw. . . ."

This is either true or false. There is no in between.

Many labor under the disadvantage of an overly active human personality. The most damaging thing we can do is to draw people to our own charms. The world is full of weak persons who long to depend upon a seemingly stronger human personality. When, inadvertently or consciously, we allow this to happen, we do great harm to those weaker persons.

This has been a problem with me. A good part of the time, I am quite sickened at my own human personality because I know myself so well. But I do have the heritage of having had parents with unusually outgoing personalities. One of the first things I remember my mother teaching me was how to make the person to whom I am saying "How do you do?" feel warm inside because I have said it. Everyone who knew my father, loved him. My mother is an exceedingly charming woman, with a way about her of making one want to be one's very best when she is around. My brother Joe and I were brought up in an atmosphere of human personality development. Whether we feel like it or not, we "go out" to people when we meet them, simply because we have been taught to do it. Twigs do get bent! And on the whole, I am grateful for this training at home. But I have been guilty of hurting people because of it. Especially if one speaks from a platform or writes books, one easily becomes distorted all out of normalcy to the public. Especially to lonely people who are seeking fulfillment in their empty lives in the questionable, but convenient method of latching onto someone who gives the appearance of a stable personality.

Sometimes, when I have snatched the controls of my own personality away from Christ (and I do!) I discover myself to be among the most unstable. But the public seldom allows a writer or a speaker to be human. And so, I have unnecessarily hurt many people who think I am something I am most certainly not on my own. I only manage my friendships

well when I face the fact (which we must all face) that
everything I have, I have been given!

We need to stay out of the Lord's glorious way. We only
block Him when we exert our own charms, however feeble
they may be. But now and then, even when we are not
blocking Him, an unhealthy, disturbed personality will at-
tach itself to us. I am sure many of you who read this page
will have experienced this kind of attachment. My instinct
is to want to get away fast and forever! And we need the
perfect perception of the Holy Spirit Himself to differentiate
between an unhealthy attachment and an honest search for
truth. Recently I was beginning to fear a wrong attachment,
when the Lord began to work and things turned out well.
This person was clinging to me *only* because she was convinced that I was convinced about Jesus Christ. She is His
now and we are good, easy friends.

Minister's wives frequently have this difficulty in their
tireless efforts to help troubled people. I have been relieved
greatly by conversations with them in the past. Relieved to
find out that there are some people who just will fasten onto
us, no matter what we do or do not do.

Jesus has said, "Feed my sheep." We must do it. But feed-
ing sheep is not done in the always well regulated restaurant
atmosphere of quiet emotions. There are deep valleys and
craggy ravines and turbulent streams and high rocks to cross
and many times, after we've crossed them we find the sheep
aren't hungry after all. They just wanted to know us better!

Actually, I don't have many close friends. I find I can no
longer afford that luxury. I travel too much for one thing.
But the main impediment to close friendships is the constant
fear that some who want to be "special" will lean on me
instead of on Jesus Christ. And I can do nothing for anyone.
My closest friends, the few to whom I would turn if I were
in trouble, are not usually my regular correspondents either!

We are really friends and our love does not need to be pumped up with letters and primed with visits and long distance telephone calls.

The Bible tells us that we are not to have "inordinate affection" for another human being. It might be well for us to take a look at Webster's definition for the word "inordinate" right here. "Not ordered or kept within bounds; unregulated, unrestrained; hence, excessive, immoderate."

I believe this Scriptural admonition concerns husbands and wives, as well as any relationship outside the marital pattern. I believe it concerns mothers and their children, too. I have come in contact with many mothers who have had "inordinate affection" for their sons or daughters. Usually it is only for one of their children. The much written about Oedipus complex (the inordinate affection of a child for the parent of the opposite sex) *should* be much written about. I know of one such instance where the son has embarked on his fourth marriage, simply because his attachment for his mother is stronger than any other.

True friendship, *controlled and regulated by the love of Christ Himself,* is the first necessary ingredient for the right parent-child relationship. For the right husband and wife relationship.

And certainly it is the first necessary ingredient for right friendships between women. Many of you would be shocked at the number of heartbroken and troubled letters I receive from Christian women who are deeply embroiled in "inordinate affection" for each other. In most cases, they believe they are remaining true to Christ because they have not become involved in what they call "immorality." But my heart aches for them, because regardless of their actual behavior, they have permitted another person to get into God's place in their lives. Certainly, I understand their heartache. Certainly, I understand how these things happen. One woman's husband was threatening to divorce her for another woman. (All persons involved were Christian believers.) Her heart was so smashed she turned to a woman friend for comfort. Later, her husband changed his mind and no longer wanted the divorce. But her attitudes and feelings toward him had changed in the meantime. She had turned to the woman friend who had comforted her. Now, he threatens divorce again. But for a different reason. He refuses to allow her close woman friend in the house. There is a dangerous triangle. And only if Christ is once more put in the center of this woman's life can tragedy be avoided.

Another woman I know writes to her woman friend every day! And if there is stormy weather and the air mails are not on schedule, she is panicky when her letter doesn't arrive. Like a lovesick school girl, she runs to a telephone and places a long distance call. At the moment, her telephone bill is far beyond her. And she is a nervous wreck, living from day to day for those beloved letters.

She *is* lovesick. And she will remain a sick woman until she remembers that her friend is not love, *God* is love. In my own life I have watched Him work wonderfully through close friendships. He reached me for Himself through a close friend. He has now sent another friend to work with me and to live with me. We all need one or two real friends in whom we can confide the deepest yearnings of our hearts. We all need companionship. We need someone to whom we don't have to explain ourselves. Someone who "gets" our humor, who loves us even when we are unlovely.

Someone upon whom we can depend in times of crisis. My associate, Rosalind Rinker, was like a rock to me during my father's illness last year. She prayed with me. She prayed with Mother. She helped us get our hasty meals together. She let me talk and talk at night after long hours at the hospital, when I was too upset to sleep. She was there in all ways. She was a real friend. To Mother and to me. And if ever I needed a friend, I needed one during those endless days and weeks while my beloved dad lay dying in a hospital.

But our friendship is on a permanent, easy, secure basis because it is not centered in us. It is centered in Jesus Christ. I am not her security and she is not mine. He is *our* security. We can fail each other but He will never fail us.

Jesus Christ is definitely in favor of close friendships. John felt so secure in his special place in the Lord's heart that he dared to write of himself as "the disciple whom Jesus loved." Guilelessly, he laid his head on Jesus' shoulder even at the supper table. Jesus Christ is not against close friendships. He is never against love. He is love! But because He is love and because He is an all-wise God, He jealously guards His central position in our lives. He isn't angry if you are centering your affections on someone else. He is grieved. Because He knows exactly how He created the moral laws which He built right into this universe. He knows that only heartache and trouble can result when we disobey. He doesn't demand the center in our lives just to prove His power. He demands it because He knows what is in man and what is in woman, and knowing this, He knows that only He is capable of coping with and satisfying our deepest longings.

If you know someone who is involved in an "inordinate affection" right now, someone who is being "excessive" and "disorderly" in the handling of her emotions, for Jesus' sake, don't condemn her! Show her quietly and lovingly that He is all in favor of love. And let her see through *your* love and understanding, that since He is love, He and He alone knows what will eventually bring her the most happiness. Actually, a woman involved in an "inordinate affection" can turn out to be an unusually strong Christian. These tendencies show a deep, deep God capacity. They show a deep, deep love capacity and this is always God capacity. Because God is love.

And He is forever mindful of all our human relationships. Not for one minute is He unaware of us. Not for one minute is He unaware of our need to love and to be loved. Time spent alone with Him, discovering His *real* intentions toward us, will inevitably result in His wooings to Himself. And when He is in charge of our emotions, they are orderly and they run smoothly. Smoothly and deeply. More deeply because like a deep, powerful river, their banks are high and regular. And like a deep river, they reach their destination.

13

The Difference Christ Makes . . .
IN YOUR REBELLIONS

13

The Difference Christ Makes...

IN YOUR REBELLIONS

If there is one among you who can honestly say she has no rebellions at all, certainly she has no need of reading further in this book.

The periods of rebellion in a Christ-controlled life may be only seconds long. But I have yet to see anyone who does not live through times of adjustment. And the very necessity for adjustment proves the presence of at least fleeting moments of rebellion.

I, for one, am a born rebel. And so, when I write that it makes all the difference in the world when Christ is in control of a naturally rebellious heart, I am speaking from my own personal experience. But I shall not stop with my experience. I am made aware daily, by mail and by conversation, that other women are rebels, too. They may not recognize themselves as such, but if we see the root of rebellion as stemming from our first mother, Eve, and if we accept rebellion as stemming from the self-protective part of our natures, we must all admit to being rebels.

Not long ago one woman told me she had grown rebellious at God because her pet prayers were not being answered. She was released from her rebellion only when she admitted she was "asking amiss."

Another wrote "I have just discovered that my heart has been rebellious ever since the birth of my dear retarded child. I called it resignation. It is really rebellion! But I am through with self-pity now. My heartache is now clothed in glory, because I have stopped rebelling and have begun to cooperate with Christ."

Another wrote: "My mother left me when I was a child. Although I had good care, I never stopped rebelling at the fact that my own mother didn't love me. But I have stopped now. Through your book *Discoveries,* I have discovered how much Christ loves me. His love melted me into being willing to see my mother again. Through talking to me, she came to know Christ, too, as her own Saviour. Mother died a few weeks ago, but our last weeks together were a miracle of love, where for so many years there was only rebellion and misunderstanding."

A dear friend of mine recently said: "Ever since I became a Christian a few years ago, I have rebelled at the idea of having to serve Christ in the usual church ways. Finally, I let this nonsense go and took a Sunday school class. When I faced them to share Jesus Christ with them the first time, their faces seemed suddenly to change before me! They seemed to glow with peace and quietness. But I know this was only true because, with my rebellion gone, He could get through me to transform them!"

Last year this letter came. "You know, Genie, that I married my husband against my better judgment. You know that sometimes I have loathed him! Before I knew Christ, I just spent my days swimming through a sea of self-pity. I still am rebellious some of the time. Not long ago I decided it must be God's will for me to leave my husband and go into full-time Christian work. I fooled myself into a sense of peace about it. Then I bought your daily devotional book *Share My Pleasant Stones.* On page 311, the Lord showed me what I had rebelled against seeing. But He showed me so clearly this time that I had to look! You wrote, 'Remaining in prison can sometimes lead to a greater fulfilling of God's purpose than for us to go free.' I am still with my husband. And the bad times still come, but they are less bad now because I am no longer rebelling against my lot in life. I have accepted it and I am trusting Christ."

A quiet, gentle lady handed me this note at a women's retreat: "I have been a missionary in Europe. Circumstances forced me to come back to America a year ago. I did not understand why I had to come back. I became rebellious and blamed everyone I could think of! Recently, the Lord has shown me that it is not the place where we serve that counts to Him. He is more concerned about my relationship to Him than about the place of my service."

Every letter that comes is not a triumphant letter, with rebellions gone.

"I am seventeen and I hate God and I hate Christians because they believe in Him. He let my mother desert me and He let my father get killed in an accident. I'm a rebel against God and I'm going to stay that way! I read in your book, *Never a Dull Moment,* about a teenager named Sue who thanks God for her heartaches. Believe me, I'll never thank Him for mine!"

Rebellious natures are not limited to teenagers.

"I am a woman 64 years old. My husband left me for another woman when I was forty. I have grown thin and old carrying my rebellion. I will have to see a bigger God than the One I see now ever to let it go!"

Life seems to be good to some and cruel to others. But

down deep inside most of us there is some human reason for rebellion. We are born with our rebellion faculties intact. Our part is to unlearn how to use them!

This may seem strange to you, but the majority of the rebellion letters which I receive are not because of desertion, or unhappy marriages, or tragic accidents. They are from Christians who harbor unconscious rebellion in their hearts against heaven and mankind because they are not in so-called full-time Christian service.

Here are just a few quotations from some of those letters:

"I have read all your books, and I know I shouldn't say I envy you, but I do. My life would work, too, if I had a chance to serve Christ as my life's work!"

"I am thirty-seven years old, am married and have a good husband and two children. But I am most miserable. God gave me an excellent singing voice and He has never given me ample opportunity to use it for His glory. I know it is a high calling to be a wife and mother, but I'm not cut out for it. I feel I am not in God's will at all. If He gave me this voice, doesn't He expect me to use it?"

Women are not the only rebels. This letter came not long ago from a Christian man with a rebellious heart.

"I have been pastor of a small church for thirteen years. The needs of my wife and son have been provided. Now, suddenly, I am positive that God is calling me into evangelism. My denomination headquarters is handling me like I'm a six-year-old. No one seems to take me seriously. I have given up my church because I felt I had to. Even the church members are complaining because they say I left them in the lurch. Everyone seems to be ganging up on me as I try to follow God's will. The utilities companies turned off our light and gas. My wife is acting like a spoiled brat because she has had to go to work to support us during this interim period when I am trying to find pulpits which will allow me to preach salvation to sinners in evangelistic meetings. I am not writing to you because of my own problems. I am writing to see if you could help me get some engagements. The more unreasonable my wife and son and friends become, the more I am determined to become an evangelist."

There *is* a "spoiled brat" involved in this man's dilemma, but it is not his wife! It is almost unbelievable that a minister could be so blind and self-deceived. He has obviously been carried away with the idea of the numbers of souls and the crowds involved in regular mass evangelism. He cannot give up the image he has built of himself as the center around which all this glamor revolves. His heart is rebellious, through and through, and the poor man is puzzled as to why God does not open doors for him. So puzzled that he wrote to ask *me* to push open a few!

New converts frequently (and understandably) get carried away with the idea of serving God in some special capacity. Frankly, it was the last thing I thought He'd ever call me to do. The fact that He did proves nothing at all. We should all consider ourselves called into full-time service, but God alone knows exactly how He means to use us. And I'm afraid unconscious rebellion at not being in the limelight is at the basis of much of the fevered agitation to get into what is known as "the Lord's work." Every Christian is in the Lord's work. Or should be. Whether you earn your living that way or not is beside the point, as I see it.

I am reasonably sure that I did not mistake His call in this way, because I am still having to surrender my public life into His Hands. Sometimes many times a day. If I were to rebel, my rebellion would go the other direction. I am utterly amazed that God should choose to place me in a public ministry. But apparently He did, and until I get the word from Him otherwise, there I will stay. However, if I had my way, I'd be alone most of the time in some well decorated

secluded little house, with no telephone and a once a week
mail delivery! There I would write books and play records
and read books and eat thick steaks and sit by an open fire
and read more books and play more records and write more
books so I could, in turn, eat more steaks. As things are, I
am only home about three months out of the year with no
fireplace!

The "ground on which you stand *is* holy ground" if you are
His. And if He is in control of you, the place where He has
put you now can be your scene of service. I believe it was
Oswald Chambers who said our tendency is to "choose the
scene of our sacrifice!" We choose what we think becomes us
most. But God has already said that His ways are higher than
ours and that His thoughts are higher than our thoughts.

And they are.

I am sure rebellion hammers at the hearts of mothers whose
children are born imperfect in some way. Deformed or retarded, deaf or blind. My friend, Dale Evans Rogers (one of
God's great women!), told me of the fight against rebellion in
her own heart when her daughter, Robin, was born a mongol-
oid. But if you have read Dale's little book, *Angel Unaware*,
you know that she exchanged rebellion for a shining acceptance of the heartbreak, and trusted God in a most amazing
way to make creative use of it. You may be one of the thousands of women who have found the way out of rebellion by
reading this lovely little book. If you are not one of those
who have read it, I urge you to do so. As you read *Angel
Unaware*, you will know that it is written by a mother who
understands your inner rebellion if your child has been born
defective. I can tell you what God will do for you, but Dale
has been in it with you.

The truly Christ-centered personality may have to resist
rebellion, but it need never fall all the way into it. We decide.
In Lima, Ohio, last year, a deeply Christian woman waited

for me after a meeting. Her face was filled with pain and anxiety. I sat down in a little side chapel alone with her. For a minute, she just swallowed her tears and then she said, "Genie, the doctors just told me today that my twelve-year-old daughter has leukemia."

My father had just died from it. She knew I would be with her in it. Leukemia in adults does not always kill as quickly as it killed my father. It usually kills youngsters in a few months. She knew this. I knew it. I said nothing at all to her. I just took her hand and we sat there bearing it together for a few minutes. Then she looked at me.

"Rebellion in my heart will do no good. I must keep my heart full of sweetness for her sake. I know this. I just thought maybe you could say something to me to help."

The woman was smiling slightly. She felt sorry for me, too. She knew I didn't have any pat answer. And I thanked God in my heart as I sat there with her that she was His. That she was willing *not* to sink into rebellion. That she really wanted a hand up out of her shock and sorrow. I sat with her a moment longer and then these words came:

"Whatever happens, I can promise you, He will be with you in it."

Oddly enough the words didn't fall flat. They soared gloriously around the room and we both prayed with hearts bubbling over with thanksgiving that what I had said was true.

He would be with her in it. As He was there in that little chapel with us then.

Whether your rebellion times spring from work you don't like, a marriage you wish you hadn't made, disobedient children, a relative in the house, death, illness, accident, or just a general feeling that you're too precious for life to treat you this way, there is but one answer.

Look at Jesus Christ. As He is.

Did anyone who has ever lived on this earth have more

reason to be rebellious than He, as they nailed Him to a Cross to crucify Him as a common criminal? He was God hanging there! How dare the very creatures whom He had created treat Him in such a ghastly manner? How dare they?

He, "the Holy One of Israel . . . high and lifted up."

Didn't Jesus Christ have every plausible reason to feel rebellion in His heart?

But what did He feel? He felt compassion! Tender, sensitive, creative, forgiving compassion.

"Father, forgive them, for they know not what they do."

If this Jesus Christ is in control of our personalities, He will never guide them toward rebellion. He permits everything that happens in your life. Rebellion at life is rebellion at God. Rebellion at God is the heart of sin. And "Jesus Christ came to earth to save sinners" from their rebellious selves!

14

The Difference Christ Makes . . .

IN YOUR SPIRITUAL LIFE

14

The Difference Christ Makes...

IN YOUR SPIRITUAL LIFE

"Dear Eugenia Price . . . I am beside myself or I wouldn't be writing this letter to you. My home is being wrecked by my constant drooping and worrying about the state of my soul! I am neglecting my husband and children.

"My husband and I attend a church where they talk all the time about being 'born again.' Together we gave our hearts to the Lord, but nothing happened. My husband doesn't worry much about it, but I do. Everyone in the church seems to look at us in a strange way because we are still doing some things which they don't approve of doing. They make me feel guilty all the time. Every time an invitation is given, I feel I should go forward again, but I have already asked Christ to come into my life and what is the point of doing it over and over? Still I am wretched. Maybe the Lord is only in my head and not in my heart. I have terrible doubts about His ever having come into my life at all. For months I have been having a dreadful mental battle. And I am no closer to loving God or having the fullness of the Spirit than before. I'm making myself sick and getting no place fast. I've been so miserable the past few months that every morning after spending most of the night wracking my brains over this thing, life looks gloomy to me and I feel I'm going out of this life as unsaved as I came into it! The preacher gives messages on the Tribulation and I get tied up in worse knots than ever, I am so scared. I've even tried visiting my non-Christian sister to get away from all that haunts me—the Bible, God, the church, the whole misery of it all! But the whole time I was afraid of hell and what was going to happen to me because I am not saved.

"Has the Lord hardened my heart? Twice this week I have asked Him again to come into my heart. I tried to witness to a friend to make myself believe it. Of course, it was a big flop. I just can't seem to receive Christ! I've ruined my home life. Can you help me?"

This dear woman's letter went on for sixteen pages of more of the same. My answer read something like this:

"My dear friend, you are caught in a negative whirl, from which you can be freed only by resolute cooperation with the Holy Spirit on your part, and a realization that Jesus Christ is tenderly concerned about you. I am entirely convinced of your sincerity. First of all, you are looking for a *feeling* of Christ's Presence in your life. No doubt, others have told you this, too. And it is true. The Bible says 'He is not the author of confusion.' But I do not put all the blame for your evident confusion entirely upon you. I think the members of your church are partly responsible for it. They haven't meant to do this, but someone at least, has shown little respect for your personality depths in attempting to force you into a mold of Christian behavior. There is a great tendency to become panic-stricken, if our own feelings of salvation do not compare in intensity or joy with those of our brothers or sisters who shout Amen at everything.

"We are not alike as people. We are all different. God recognizes this, but people usually do not. One thing I know: If you received Christ into your heart sincerely, *He came!* And He never comes just to the head. He comes to the whole person. Some of us are constituted so that we do not have immediate feelings. From what you tell me of your background, you had never heard of being 'born again' until you began to attend this church. It is all so new to you and people are so much easier to see, and ministers are so much easier to hear than God, that you allow them to muddle you where God is concerned!

"Jesus Christ said, 'Him that cometh to me I will in no wise cast out.' You must decide whether you believe Him or not. Your problem is exactly here. Either you believe that He meant what He said or not. I see nothing in His Personality that would make me think that He would make an exception of you! He also said, 'I, if I be lifted up . . . . will draw *all* men unto me.' Peter wrote that 'God is not willing that *any* should perish.' Frankly, I question that Christ Himself was lifted up to you. I believe perhaps a plan of salvation, with an insurance policy against an unpleasant after-life, may have been 'lifted up' rather than the great Heart of the Saviour, Himself. I have no way of knowing this, but from my own experience and from the experiences of many, many others whom I have known, once He, Himself, has been 'lifted up,' our hearts are permanently hooked by His love!

"If I were you, I'd leave the 'Tribulation' entirely in His hands. Whatever He does, whenever He does it, will be the loveliest and the fairest and the perfect thing. It has to be, because He is God, and 'God is love!' You are ruining your todays by being unduly anxious over a nebulous, future tomorrow. The walk with Jesus Christ is a minute by minute walk with a Living Person. He Himself said, 'Sufficient unto the day is the evil thereof.' I think He was thinking particu-

larly about persons like yourself, who have a tendency to
carry tomorrow today. No one can whip up a feeling of love
for a stranger. If you will turn to Christ right now (He's right
there in the room, you know!) and say simply, 'All right, Lord,
You teach me what You're really like,' I believe at least some
of your panic will drop away.

"Don't expect the damage from all this negative thinking
to vanish at once. Our minds are not constructed that way.
But begin to walk with Him. Talk to Him all day long as
you work. Force yourself to sing songs about Him. Just repeat
His Name over and over and over. Tell Him you love Him
whether you feel love or not.

"Salvation is not a process which particularly concerns us.
That is His department! And He is a God of His Word. Above
all, stop trying to imitate the good brothers and sisters in
your church. They mean well. But my advice to you is, be
yourself. And let Jesus Christ be Himself in you. Of course,
He has *not* hardened your heart. What a foolish thing for
God to do after the great lengths to which He went on the
Cross to make it possible for us to come to Him!"

I have not quoted all of her letter, nor all of mine to her.
But, although hers is an extreme case, it is not an unusual one.

I am pleased with this opportunity to share my conviction
that we have horribly and shamefully complicated the very
Truth which Christ brought into the world! The troubled
letters ramble on for pages about the inability of the person
who is writing the letter to lay hold of some aspect of the life
in Christ. They are filled with confusion about a theological
point or they are packed with tangled emotions and helplessly
clouded with man made complications. These people are trying so frantically to lay hold of Him that they miss completely
the *fact* that He has laid hold of them or they wouldn't be
giving it a thought!

God paid a visit to this earth in the Person of Jesus of

Nazareth in order to do away with the necessity for emotional binges and special visions. He came to simplify Himself so that the most limited among us could know Him and know Him intimately and well.

I now see that much of my own spiritual life has been a pathetic self-effort. Because I now see this, I can certainly identify with all of you who are still under the impression that the Bible is written for Christians in order to persuade them to reach greater heights. The Bible is an invitation to *sinners* to come and take full advantage of the poured out life of God Himself in Christ. And to come daily.

We are forever trying to keep up with the Joneses spiritually. I have tied someone else's spiritual fruits on my tree until I am exhausted with picking them up off the ground, where they surely fall every time life gives me a blow. The fruits of the Spirit are merely evidences of Christ's life within us. When we act in a Christian manner, this is not because we have great light and spiritual perception. This is not because of our great obedience and the perfection of our lives. This is not because we keep a regular quiet time every day and give beyond our tithe. When we act in a Christian manner, it is *only* because we who are sinners have chosen to let Christ act like Himself through us!

Another letter also caused me great heartache. This person had been confused by my book *Early Will I Seek Thee*. In this book I wrote of the fact that we *are* crucified with Christ. And although many of you have written that it was through that book that the Holy Spirit made this truth clear, one woman, at least, was highly confused.

She wrote, "How can I die to self? Must this happen before Christ comes in or after He comes?"

We *never* die to self!

Paul tells us we are to "die daily," but he says nothing whatever about a once for all suicidal act on our part. He tells us, rather, that when we lean firmly upon the strength of Christ, we realize that we have already been crucified with Him. To me, this is a moment by moment realization.

In untheological terms it means this to me: Once, before I received Christ, I could not control myself at all times. Now that I have received Him, I can, if I choose to do it, place constantly under His control the stubborn, disobedient, human being that I am. I can be the same as dead to myself and alive to the very Personality of Christ.

Many women write to me about their "lack of faith." One woman wrote: "I am trying to have faith. I am trying to please Christ. But it seems a losing battle."

My good friend, Wesley Nelson, pastor of the Mission Covenant Church in Oakland, California, has written a little book which I urge you to read. Only recently, after years in the ministry, did he allow Christ to simplify things as He so longs to do. This book, *Captivated By Christ* (published by the Christian Literature Crusade), is a disarmingly honest and provocative telling of this new experience of the simplicity of Christ Himself in Wesley Nelson's own life. I'm quoting now directly from his passage on faith: "The first obstacle that must fall is a mistaken idea about faith. We have a tendency to think of faith as a commendable human trait, like courage or trustworthiness. It is often looked upon as an attitude of heart or state of mind which some people have and others lack. Those who seem to have it are said to be 'religiously inclined.' When we define faith in this way, we immediately set up a division among human beings, so that some find it easy to be religious and others tend to consider themselves quite incapable of an active religious interest.

"Jesus cuts right through this mistaken idea. He does not define faith as some inherent quality which men possess, by which they may unlock the door to spiritual truth. He does not say, 'Faith is the way.' He says, 'I am the way. . . .'

"When the good news of Christ (Himself) is unfolded before us and we allow ourselves to see what it really means, we are captivated by it. When this happens, *faith is born*."

You and I experience faith as an inevitable *result* of discovering what Jesus Christ is really like! When we know a person, if that knowing relaxes us into trust, then we have faith in that person.

Another deeply troubled woman wrote: "Can anyone receive Jesus Christ at any old time or in any old place?"

My answer is an unequivocal Yes.

I do not for one minute discount the fact that the Holy Spirit must reveal the true identity of God to us. *But* is there a possible contradiction among the Persons of the Godhead? If the Father God "loved the world" so much that He would send His Son to die for it, does it make any sense whatever that either the Son or the Holy Spirit would love the same world any less than the Father loves it? And doesn't it follow with lovely logic that the Holy Spirit is *always* willing to convince human beings of their need of a Saviour and to reveal Him? If "God is not willing that any should perish," do you think the Holy Spirit is willing for some to remain in darkness?

God gave us minds and He has every right to expect us to use them. When we refuse to be basic with God and do some honest thinking for ourselves in His Presence and in the revealed light of the Scriptures, we fall into stupid confusion about Him. We complicate the beautiful simplicity of God's visit to this earth beyond all recognition. I fully respect and believe the prophetic teachings of the Bible. But as Christians, our responsibility is to follow Jesus Christ in childlike obedience and simplicity. It is not up to us to cloud the issue of Christ Himself by trying to understand the ramifications and the obscurities of the "Tribulation."

He is God. Let Him handle the things that are His to

handle. He will do it perfectly. That includes *everything* at
the time of His return.

Another highly intelligent young woman wrote: "I began
to doubt that I was a Christian during my freshman year at
college. When I was a junior in college, I had an experience
with Christ which gave me peace for a time. For most of the
remainder of my college days, my mind was full of uncer-
tainty, though most of the time I was active in religious
groups. Since college, although I am in a responsible church
job, and although my family has always been considered religious, I must admit that Jesus Christ is not real to me! I stand,
at this writing, unable to move one way or another. Afraid to
look long enough to see myself as I really am. Wanting to find
reality and not wanting to. However, your books, *Discoveries*,
The Burden is Light, and *Early Will I Seek Thee*, have so
captivated my thoughts that I find myself longing to know
Him as you know Him. I do not mean that I want your particular experience. After all, I am I and you are you. But these
books have convinced me that Jesus Christ is real to you. I'm
tired singing solos about Him in church, tired having people
compliment me, saying I am so sincere. Then I come home and
can't even pray! I know God exists, but I can't get Him tied
up with Jesus Christ somehow."

This letter interested me greatly. Actually, this girl was
much closer to reality than she realized. My answer contained
some of what I will have to say to you in chapter 16. To
her, God and Jesus Christ were two different people. When,
in reality they are One. She admitted in a part of her letter
which I did not quote for you that perhaps she was afraid of
the great adventure of belonging entirely to Jesus Christ. She
alone must decide about this. The familiar, "safe" nest of
conventional religion in which she had grown up, still feels
quite comfortable to her. I understand this. But I am also
grateful that my books stirred her up! No one's spiritual life

works if one is clinging to the warm, familiar, nest, however cozy it may seem. Or however airless and stuffy. When Jesus Christ invites us to follow Him, we have to let Him decide where we are going.

Another woman, a successful social worker, described this "familiar nest" habit well in my first letter from her. "I know a new life has begun for me, but the habit of being an in-betweener and the much practiced skill of rationalizing makes uncloaking sin in my life a slow business." I am delighted to tell you that this woman is now free! She became convinced once and for all that Jesus Christ, through the Holy Spirit, would enable her to break her old thought patterns. In a later letter she wrote: "I can see why Jesus hated hypocrisy! He hates to have us bound. And it is terribly binding. Being critical, giving way to frustration and irritation and then going into discouragement are the inevitable fruits of bad habits of thinking and lack of the knowledge of who Christ really is! I am through with all of them and just now beginning the shining new (all new) adventure of faith, with Him."

Right here in your reading, I would like to ask you to turn back and reread chapter three and chapter four on the conscious and subconscious mind.

Supposing that you have done this, you will remember that in chapter three on the conscious mind, we saw that we do control what is dropped into our subconscious minds. With your conscious mind, you can form the habit of daily Bible reading. No one can make this decision but you. But you can do it. And no chapter on the spiritual life would be complete without a reminder that, even on the days when the Bible seems to make no sense at all to you, with your conscious mind as you read it, you are dropping the written down Word of God into your subconscious! When you force yourself to sing a song of praise to the Saviour, even when you don't feel like it, you are dropping the words of that song into your subconscious mind. You are building a storehouse there for future use in emergency situations. If you and I stock the "baskets" of our subconscious minds with the things of God, we can absolutely depend upon the Holy Spirit's exploding them into our conscious minds when we need them! One woman, whose husband had been killed suddenly before her eyes in an accident, was the inspiration of a retreat I attended some years ago. I asked her how she accounted for the peace and calm she was showing in Christ. I knew Christ was responsible for it, but I wanted to know how she had laid hold of His peace. The accident had happened a short month before I met her. She looked at me and said, "Genie, the only answer I know is that all through the years, even when I didn't want to, I read my Bible every day. The Lord must have managed to store it up for me somewhere and it is holding now."

Her subconscious mind was stored with Truth. And it was there to sustain her when she needed it so desperately.

Our spiritual lives are not dependent upon our daily devotional times. They are dependent upon Christ Himself. But time spent alone with Him, allowing Him to speak to us through the Bible, is our access to His grace. Grace is always flowing toward us. Always. Our part is to put out our cups to receive it. I like to think of my own devotional hours as receiving hours.

But this receiving must not end when we close our Bibles. The normal, relaxed Christian life is one that is regulated by a definite rhythm like breathing: Receiving and responding. Receiving and responding.

Perhaps many of you feel that your prayer life is the weakest part of your Christian life. It well may be. I know I considered mine weak for many years. And yet we make a horrible mistake when we think of prayer as separate from our Christian walk. When we walk with a human friend, talking to that friend is an integral part of the walk.

If you have reread chapter four on the subconscious mind, you have the story of Marian freshly in your mind. In telling that story, I described a natural, conversational prayer through which Christ touched this fearridden young woman and healed her.

This easy, natural, unstilted conversational praying has greatly changed my own prayer life. I have never been formal or conventional with God. I didn't hear a prayer from the age of fifteen to thirty-three. I really had no one to imitate. But through praying with my close friend and associate, Miss Rosalind Rinker, I have begun to understand the amazing freedom waiting for us all in conversational prayer with another person. A little over a year ago as I write this book, she came to live and work with me. And I have freely reaped the reward of her long, sometimes painful years of breaking out of the stuffy, conventional prayer pattern. Rosalind was a missionary in China praying with a close friend, years ago, when God began to set her free in her prayer life. And I would indeed be highly unfair to you if I did not tell you that you may discover all that she and I know of this easy, Spirit-guided prayer freedom in a new book which she is writing as I write this one. It will be called simply *Prayer-Conversing with God* (Zondervan). In *Woman to Woman* I have tried to recommend to you certain books which have helped me. This one is a "must" for anyone (man or woman) who longs for more simplicity and honesty and results in prayer. I live with Rosalind Rinker. I can tell you that she lives an authentic, direct, childlike Christian life. You will sense this when you read her little book, *Prayer-Conversing with God,* and from it you will learn how we approach our own prayer times.

From some of the letters which I have shared with you in this chapter, I am sure you agree that the basic answer to them all is Jesus Christ Himself. When a woman is anxious and uneasy about her salvation, let her remember that He is handling that end of it. Her part is to *respond* to the Person of Jesus Christ Himself. If she trusts Him and if she stops agitating long enough to think clearly, she will be content to leave salvation which is so beyond her, in His dear hands. If her prayer life is shallow, let her remember to whom she is praying.

Jesus Christ is "the same yesterday, today and forever." It is our circumstances and our emotions which change. God created our emotions, too. And He created them with the ability to change! If He hadn't we could neither weep nor laugh. We would be automatons. But He has made us people, with longings and desires which we express and give vent to through our emotions. I try to remember that like the weather, my emotions change. They are apt to get my attention simply because they have changed. But, since I do control my conscious mind, I can deliberately turn that mind *from* my emotions to Jesus Christ Himself, who never changes.

He, then, *is* our Christian life. I can look past my swaying emotions to Him, knowing that He will always take even my stormy feelings into gentle consideration. "He remembereth that we are dust."

I have been greatly helped in my own Bible study by using, along with the King James version, the newer translations: Phillips, Berkeley, Williams. And I am most enthusiastic about the Amplified New Testament (Zondervan). It is interesting to know that most of the work in this excellent version was done by a woman, Frances E. Siewert, who spent most of her long life preparing it. We owe her a debt of love and gratitude.

15

The Difference Christ Makes . . .

IN YOUR UNDERSTANDING

OF HUMAN NATURE

15

The Difference Christ Makes...
IN YOUR UNDERSTANDING
OF HUMAN NATURE

"I'm glad to discover that Christians are *people*. At this retreat this week, I've learned that we don't have to brace ourselves and be 'Christians!'"

These words were spoken by an intelligent, attractive woman in her thirties, who had waited until next to the last day of the retreat to become a follower of Jesus Christ. She had agreed to come, out of respect for a friend, who is an integral part of our Cedar Lake, Indiana, retreat every year. But all week long, she had stayed on the fringes and I knew that inwardly at least, she maintained a raised eyebrow about all Christians. Happily, during this one week out of the year, my meetings are under no organizational auspices. We meet merely as a group of people who see their need for a better look at Jesus Christ as He really is. We don't go overboard on special music, we don't preach, we laugh a lot, and sometimes we weep. We don't attempt to pour the personalities of new Christians into a mold. Everyone participates. I have intentionally kept this week apart for those dear pagans and recent converts who, like myself only a few years ago, are convinced that Christians have to be peculiar and eccentric and stuffy.

But Christians are people.

And I believe one of the reasons why outsiders get a distorted idea about us is because of our appalling lack of understanding of *human nature* as it really is.

Those Christians who go about spouting "humble phrases" in which they piously speak of themselves as "worms," and are unable to carry on a conversation about any other subject but religion, are damaging to the cause of Christ. In the first place, they are being dreadfully "human" when they run themselves down in order to convince others of their "humility." This is, in reality, ego at its flaming worst. Jesus Christ did not die to save worms. He died to save people created in His image.

Haven't you heard the reply, when you have given an honest compliment, "Oh, I did nothing. I'm just a nobody. The Lord did it all"? Look at that sentence. There are *two* references to *I* and only one to the Lord! When we run ourselves down on the phony premise that we are glorifying the Lord, we are actually only calling attention to ourselves. A long time ago, the Lord informed me that when someone compliments me, I am merely to be a polite human being and reply, "Thank you." Nothing more. If Christ is really in control of our lives, we don't need to remind people that He is. It shows. We can go on about His business, mainly ignoring ourselves. No need to praise ourselves. No need to run ourselves down.

The Bible says that we are to be a "peculiar people." But the dictionary definition of "peculiar" is "to be owned." We are to be owned by Jesus Christ and relax about trying to convince people of our piety.

This quick-thinking young woman had watched us all during the entire week of the retreat. She recognized her own humanity and longed for the companionship of other people like herself. She discovered during the week that here at least fifty-five Christians lived together for seven days and acted like *people.*

She began to feel at home with us. And certainly, except for the fact that until nearly the last day she had not accepted Christ as her Saviour, indeed, we all *were* just like her. She was a sinner who had not yet put her faith in Christ. We were sinners who had done it and were coming to Him daily for further cleansing.

Human nature is not a loathsome thing. When the Bible tells us that in our "flesh dwells no good thing," this does not mean that we have no inherent human generosity or kindness. No pleasant traits at all. It merely means that "in our flesh" until Christ comes to indwell it, is no righteousness of the caliber of the righteousness of God. The Bible infers that in human nature *is* a kind of righteousness. But then it realistically clarifies the matter by informing us that "all our righteousnesses are as filthy rags" beside the righteousness of God Himself.

Christian human nature has a right to dream and plan and think. Many Christians are so afraid that someone won't think they operate entirely on divine guidance, that they become stiff and unsociable and vague. I remember hearing about a conversation between a young Bible school student and a friend of mine. My friend, an older man, who was a brand new Christian, was having dinner with the young fellow when he spotted some luscious looking pie on the counter. "Hey, I think I'll have some of that chocolate pie," my friend said casually. The tense, fearfully pious young man fell silent a moment, looked as vague and remote as a Thurber drawing of a sheep dog, and eventually muttered, "I was just asking the Lord if it is His will for me to have a piece, too."

My friend, the new Christian, almost left the fold in dismay!

And I can't say that I blame him.

God has no plans whatever for making us *unnatural*. He is interested in giving us access to the *supernatural*. But this is a different thing.

The Lord *is* intensely interested in every small thing which we do. Jesus told us that "the very hairs of (our) heads are numbered." I rest in this. But when a Christian is living in fellowship with God, his human personality begins to resemble Christ. And as the years go on, he finds it less and less necessary to ask for definite guidance about little things. If you know your husband well and have lived with him for years, you no longer need to ask him what he likes for dinner. You know. Because you know your husband.

When we know Christ personally, we can walk with Him in a quiet, intimate certainty. His own human personality must have been lovable. People flocked to Him. Not once did Jesus Christ do the eccentric. He was all sanity. He was an easy Person to know. And to love. What an injustice we do Him now, when we who know Him go doggedly along acting according to our own Christian images of our pious selves! In every case Christianity gets the blame. And when Christianity is blamed, so is Christ Himself.

Many who feel themselves to be of the highest "spiritual caliber," are seemingly blind to the true nature of human beings. And it is a constant amazement to me that this type of blindness is often found among the conservative, evangelical Christians.

For example, when you, as a Christian, are shocked at *anything* anyone does, you are blind to the true nature of man. The Bible says that Jesus "knew what was in man." He was merely seeing men as they were, while He hung on the Cross. It required no special allotment of divine forgiveness for Jesus Christ to pray, "Father, forgive them, for they know not what they do." In His very words as He prayed from the Cross for their forgiveness, He bothered, even in His agony, to express His understanding of human nature to us! ". . . they know not what they do." And yet, we look at the unconverted son-in-law who drinks and we are shocked. We somehow think he should not drink, just because he's married to such a sweet girl. Jesus didn't pray, "Father, forgive them, because I am such a spiritual Saviour." He said, "Father, forgive them *for they know not what they do.*"

We Christians must not get so other-worldly that we leave this world behind to destroy itself. We must be patient with the dreams and hopes and desires of human nature. We must look for the positive qualities in everyone. But somehow, something must wake us up to the fact that reality *is* reality. And when you, as a Christian, expect your son-in-law, who is not a Christian, to be different in any way from just the way he is (without Christ), then you are saying that the "Cross of Jesus Christ is much ado about nothing." We must not expect non-believers to act as though they are believers!

We must be startled into realizing that we diminish the necessity for Christian faith when we expect too much of those who do *not* have it.

Certainly, the self-righteous attitude proves that we do *not* understand human nature as it really is. It declares only that because it would make life less shockable or easier for you, these persons simply shouldn't be this way. Constantly I stand amazed at the Christians who click their tongues at the millions of gallons of alcoholic beverages which are consumed in America. Why are they surprised? The people who consume it excessively don't know Christ! Are we crusading for improved human nature, or are we crusading for human nature to recognize its need of the Saviour's Nature?

Over and over again, I hear careless Christians speak of those outside Christ as "they." Not long ago I heard a much loved Christian speaker telling the story of how he tried to lead someone to Christ. I know the temptation to "get a laugh" from an audience, but when we yield to it in this way, we are making fun of someone for whom Christ died, and we set ourselves up as superior beings. This speaker was explaining how he brought the conversation around to Christ. "You know, *they* are pretty smart! We have to be smart, too, or *they'll* outwit us. And believe me, *they* can be tricky." His good fundamental audience chuckled obligingly and I wanted to cry. This man did not realize that he could have hurt the two hundred non-Christians who were in his audience. And most deplorable of all, I think, was the smug atmosphere which swept over the mainly Christian group. They reacted as though *they* were somehow different from *them*. In the smiles at his quip, I saw superiority. I saw self-approval. The last two expressions which should ever show on the faces of men and women who have truly faced their own need of a Saviour.

How different was this man who spoke from the one whom he relegated to the nether-world of "unsaved *theys*"? No different at all! The speaker had simply united his helpless, sinful human nature to the sinless Nature of Christ. The other man had not. Otherwise, they were just the same.

Is self-pity sin? Yes, it is. It is as far removed from the uncomplaining, unself-pitying attitude of God as He hung on the Cross as any attitude could possibly be. And yet, is there one Christian among us who has not for a time, at least, felt sorry for herself? For himself? Is excessive drinking a sin? Yes. But what is the difference in the basic *human nature* of the self-pitying Christian and the self-pitying alcoholic?

Is prejudice a sin? Yes, it is. But is there one among us who has never, even for a period, held prejudice closely to her heart, as she attempts to justify it by social conditions or background or some equally clever rationalization?

The crooked, non-Christian·politician in your town may hold bitter race prejudice in his heart. But if you hold it, too, how different are you from him in your *human* nature?

Recently in a Chicago paper, I read this striking short news brief: "A big share of responsibility for the world's racial and social evils must be laid at the church's doorstep. Dr. E. H. Schalkhauser told a National Lutheran Evangelism conference the unwanted bundle will remain there until the church learns to practice what it preaches about salvation and redemption. Even though many church members 'go through the motions of regular worship on Sunday mornings and hold the correct doctrinal beliefs,' he said, 'many souls are being alienated from God forever because their cultural prejudices have been nursed so long that the prospect of total spiritual integration in heaven is a revolting thought.'"

This man struck a deep note. And I'm sure it strikes deep into the heart of God, too.

Many of us who are willing to fight over the inspiration of the Scriptures, live in direct opposition to what these Scriptures say. The Bible says we are to love our neighbors as ourselves. One woman I know, who is a notorious defender of the Bible, refuses to allow her neighbor in her home if the neighbor is drinking. Is she fulfilling the law of love, according to the Scriptures? (Any alcoholic who hangs around a Christian is in his or her heart seeking Christ.)

Once and for all we must get it straight that human nature is human nature and we all have it. A pathetically small percentage of the human race has received the Nature of Christ *into* that human nature. But, even so, we must under all circumstances accept people as being just people. One of the greatest injustices we can do our fellow man is either to expect too much·or too little of him. God will give us the courage and the wisdom and the ability to accept him exactly as he is.

It is more difficult, somehow, to accept the faulty *human nature* of a professing Christian. If a Christian stubs his spiritual toe and it gets found out, all manner of chaos breaks loose. And certainly, I believe strongly that we should live open, obedient lives. We do have the reputation of Jesus Christ in our human hands wherever we go. But by bitter experience I have learned that most Christians won't allow me just to be "people." And sometimes I prove my human nature by rebelling against it. But it is nevertheless true, that if someone who is known as a responsible Christian does or says a thing which is a blow to other Christians, the "pious" fur flies. And yet, the Lord told us firmly that we are not to judge one another.

I have, in two particular instances, discovered unChristian attitudes and actions in two Christian leaders. But I thanked God from my heart that I knew they were just people, and I thanked Him for reminding me through their confidence in me, that I was just like them, too. If we accept Christian believers as being mere human beings, who have linked their lives to the Life of the Saviour, but who are still Christians in the making, we will do them a great justice. If we expect them to be supermen and superwomen, we diminish the need for Calvary in their lives.

Anyone can be a Christian. Anyone can act like a Christian. Not because of what we are, in our human nature, but because of what Jesus Christ is like in His God Nature.

In the next chapter, we will take a direct look at the Nature of God. Because surely, it is only in knowing what He is like that we can accept ourselves as we are. If your personality is directly under the control of Christ, you have access to His estimate of your own human nature. You have access to His estimate of the human nature of those you love. And His estimate of human nature neither minimizes nor exalts. He sees realistically, because He Himself is reality.

16

The Difference Christ Makes . . .

IN YOUR UNDERSTANDING
OF GOD'S NATURE

16

The Difference Christ Makes...

IN YOUR UNDERSTANDING

OF GOD'S NATURE

"I'm afraid to give over my whole life to Christ. I'm afraid of what He might ask me to do."

"If I surrender my entire personality to Christ, how do I know He won't cripple one of my children? So many dreadful things seem to happen to Christians and they are supposed to rejoice in it. I couldn't do this if God harmed one of my children."

"If I give over the controls of my life to Jesus Christ, how do I know He won't send me to some dreary foreign mission post?"

"I'm afraid to surrender to Christ because He might ask me to speak before crowds as He has asked you to do."

These are just a few of the objections to the committed life which I have picked up along the way of my travels and in the daily perusal of my mail.

In each case, these objections show a glaring lack of understanding of what God is really like!

Certainly He often asks us to do difficult things, but if He is God and if He knows the end from the beginning and if He created us in the first place, doesn't it make sense that only He knows exactly how to guide us? Of course, each objection is voiced by a woman who has not tried Him fully. No one who has, gives much thought to what He might do with her life. Invariably, even when the years are filled with hardship, in the minds of those who are wholly His there arises no question but that He will get them through it. Questions often arise in times of rebellion as to *how* He will do it, but the familiar "if" of the uncommitted is seldom in evidence. This does not mean that fully committed Christians are never discouraged or confused or in doubt. But the doubts seem to concern God's methods, not His character.

One woman wrote: "How do I know that God will not take my husband as He took Betty Elliot's husband? After all, my husband is just a businessman. And Betty's husband was in God's service. If He took Jim Elliot, what guarantee do I have that He would not take my husband?"

Here again is an appalling lack of knowledge of what God is really like. The religious philosophies of the East have made sharp inroads into Christian thinking. The law of Karma implies that we are treated by God according to our deserts. This is not dealing with reality. Jesus Christ, and only Jesus Christ, deals with life as it is. Nowhere in the Christian philosophy do we find indication that God blesses or protects according to our merits. Certainly if this were true, He would have protected His own Son from the Cross! Christianity deals with life as it is. Not as it should be. If we read our Bibles, asking the Holy Spirit to give us insight into man and God as they *are,* we will find that insight. It is certainly there.

In nothing that God does is He limited by our earthly

span of years. He is working from an eternal, over-all pattern which only God and those who have gone to be with Him can see. There isn't a human mind brilliant enough, nor a human heart spiritually enlightened enough to be able to see God's entire plan.

The Christian life is a life of faith. And faith is not, as we have already seen, given to some and not given to others. Faith is merely the natural *result* of knowing what God is like. If we know Him, then we automatically trust Him to do what He knows to be the best possible thing in our particular circumstance.

It does no good whatever to tell a woman who is afraid that God might cripple her child that she has no right to question God. In one sense we have every right to question Him. I think God is pleased when an honest man or woman confronts Him with honest questions. And the reason He is pleased is because He knows what He is like. He knows His intentions toward the whole human race. He knows that He can stand the test of our questioning.

Perhaps we should look for a moment right here at the question which has been on the lips of mankind for most of mankind's existence: Does God send all tragedy? In my own heart the answer to this profound question is no.

I doubt if anyone has a total answer. But the very question mark itself can be caused to drop away, *if* we will give ourselves a chance to look at God as He really is in Jesus Christ.

Some of you who read this book may not be convinced yet that God did visit this earth in the Person of Jesus of Nazareth. To you I recommend the reading of Dr. J. B. Phillips' books, *Your God Is Too Small* and *When God Became Man* (Macmillan). But whether or not it has become clear to you, He did reveal Himself wholly only in Jesus Christ. It was on this point that I was able to give my life to Him. If God

and Jesus Christ are one and the same, then I must follow
God. And through every year of my Christian life, I have
been following God *because* I now know Him to be One
with Jesus Christ. All that could be contained of God in a
human being came to dwell among us when Jesus came.
When I look at Christ, I am looking at God Himself. "I and
the Father are one."

So that anyone who is afraid of a hidden fiendish side
of God, will continue to be, *until* that person knows Jesus
Christ. Can you imagine Jesus Christ crippling a child? All
of His earthly days were spent in healing! Did Jesus Christ
send the crippling disease just so He could show off His
own healing power? This is absurd even to consider. Our
God is a God of wholeness. For some reason which we cannot fully understand now, He allows disease. But each time
I am in conversation with someone on this point, I seem
to become more and more convinced that we must not ask
for a pat answer. I am not convinced of this because I follow a fearful, tyrant God who shuts off my aching "why"
simply because He's God and I have no right to question
Him. I am convinced because more and more I see Him as
a totally redemptive God, who is minute by minute working
out a great eternal purpose. He is not limited to our earthly
lives and neither are we!

Just recently I sat in a minister's study before the evening
service where I was to speak. He told me of a tragedy in
one of the families in his congregation. The son was forced
to come back from the mission field after having been there
only three months, because his fifty-two-year-old father
dropped dead suddenly from a heart attack. The mother was
hospitalized also with a severe heart condition. Quietly, the
devout minister was exploring God's purpose in so much
tragedy. The father had been one of the strong members
of the church. The boy had just entered the Lord's service.

The mother lay ill. When the minister asked me what I thought about it, I said this: "I'm not sure God caused any of this. Certainly He allowed it. But certainly He allows sin! God didn't create sin. He died in order to be able to redeem us from it. I am able to keep my heart quiet in the face of these blows life hands us only by keeping my entire attention focused on the *Nature* of Jesus Christ Himself."

Over and over as my own father lay suffering so horribly during the days before his death, I was kept from asking why simply because of the time and effort I had spent during the last few years in order to find out what Jesus Christ is really like. Many times I had to remind myself that Jesus had so completely identified with me in my heartache that He had even asked my "why" for me from the Cross! So, if your own heart cries "why" at God, Christ Himself holds your answer. He is not shocked or offended at your cry. He has already asked, "My God, my God, why hast thou forsaken me?"

He knows.

Somehow, somewhere in the dark recesses of the human heart, there lies a deep suspicion of God. This must bring Him great pain. In His written-down Word He tells us that His intentions toward us are the highest and most peaceful. "I know the thoughts that I think toward you, saith the Lord, thoughts of peace and not of evil, to give you an expected end."

The end is already in His mind. He, Himself, is the end. "I am the beginning and the end," Jesus said. And yet there is within us all the natural bent to expect the worst of God.

If we look at human history, this bent is understandable. Not because God has intended human history to turn out as it has, but because so few persons who have made human history have bothered to find out what God is really like! If more had discovered Him as He is, human history would have been a different story. We who are living through the twentieth century are not experiencing the results of God's Nature when we look at the tragedy and heartbreak and tyranny in the world. We are experiencing the consequences of human nature lived without contact with God from our side.

God did not strike Betty Elliot's beloved Jim with a savage's spear. The fear and distrust and darkness in the heart of the savage struck him. And here we come to the proof of the glorious fact that even when sin strikes its darkest blow, God, because He is forever a Redeemer God, will make good, creative use of the blow! Hasn't God made magnificent use of the tragedy in the jungle when the five missionaries were murdered by the very savages they longed to reach with the Good News of Love? Just as He turned the world's greatest tragedy, Calvary, into the world's greatest victory, so He has turned that tragedy in the jungle to victory. Not only triumph for the cause of Christ, but triumph in the midst of heartache in the torn lives of the widows left behind. Betty Elliot would be the first to agree that the death of her Jim was not wasted.

It could have been. But nothing needs to be wasted when Jesus Christ is in command of the situation and of the personalities of those involved in it.

It is this deep tendency of the human heart to suspect God which prompts questions such as those shared at the beginning of this chapter. "How do I know God won't send me to a foreign field?" "How do I know God won't make me speak before people?" If God sends you to a foreign field, He will go with you, and before you are sent, you can depend on it that He will create such a love in your heart for the people to whom He is sending you, and such a desire to go, that you will scarcely be able to wait to get there.

If He "makes you speak before crowds of people," He will

enable you to do it. He will give you His love and concern for the people. He will enable you to overcome your shyness or rebellion. Many times I have arrived at the door of the church or public building where I am to speak, deeply rebellious at having to go at all. But inevitably when I stand up, I am enabled to say what He has given me to say.

It's true God may ask you to do hard things. But He asks us to do nothing which He Himself will not support.

When we question God in this way, it is only darkness or disorderly thinking on our part. We are not thinking through to the very Nature of God Himself. We are woolgathering. We are just wondering if God will turn out to adjust Himself to us! No, He can't do this. He is a holy God. But He will come to live right in your mortal body and enable you to adjust to Him. He will never ask you to do anything which He knows you cannot do, with His life operative in you.

Another question as old as the heart of man: Does God punish by affliction? As clearly as I am able to see, no. He punishes by love. It is His love and longsuffering which cause us real pain. The kind of pain which brings us to repentance. To the point of true faith. I do not fear God's punishment by tragedy when I am disobedient. But I do fear His punishment by love. The severest punishment of Peter's entire life must have been the moment after he had denied Jesus three times in a row. It was then that "the Lord turned and looked upon Peter," and "Peter went out, and wept bitterly." Love Himself had "looked upon Peter," and it broke his heart.

Our various doctrinal differences often seem to cloud the true Nature of God. Not long ago I received a most interesting but troubled letter from a young woman who had been confused by two incidents in my own life. In my autobiography, *The Burden Is Light*, she had read the chapter "How Great Is That Darkness," in which I told of emerging from a stormy dark period, some four or five years after my conversion. Then in 1958 *Christian Life* magazine published an article written by Dr. V. Raymond Edman, which gave another account (with many quotes from me) concerning still another emerging from still another period of great darkness. This one three years later. Here is a portion of her letter: "In the chapter in *The Burden Is Light* you explained so clearly about giving up the right to yourself. Now, I am really confused, because in the *Christian Life* article the content seems to be identical, but the second giving up didn't happen until later. I may be awfully dense, but I'm mixed up about it. Did you discover that you really hadn't given up your rights to yourself after all? What do you call these experiences? Or do we need to call them anything?"

The remainder of her letter showed clearly that she was fearful something like this would happen to her.

I was well aware that this type of confusion could follow Dr. Edman's article, and for the rest of you who may have been mixed up, this is the way I understand it. Once more, we lack knowledge of God's true Nature when we fall into pits of depression at the dark periods which come to all of God's people. There is one baptism, but many fillings, we are told. I do not profess to be an expert theologian. I have simply followed Christ according to the light He has given me. And I have never been much concerned about what certain differing groups would label my various and varied spiritual experiences. No love life runs smoothly all the time. The Christian life is a life of love. I trust my Loved One now because my faith in Him has been strengthened with every emergence from every dark or dry period in my Christian life.

Here again, even though we don't recognize it as such, is a manifestation of that deep tendency to suspect Him. If we learn that someone whom we admire, or who has helped us spiritually, has taken a nose dive, we are crushed Or at least confused. And we begin to wonder if Christ is going to let this happen to us, too!

Yes, He probably will.

Not to punish you, but simply because He will at all times act exactly like God. Jesus Christ is not only the Saviour God, He is also the Creator God. "Without Him was not anything made that was made." We have already spoken of the fact that He created our minds and He works with them according to the way He created them and according to what He knows we can take in at the moment. I have found the Christian life does not build regularly from any pat format. God always acts according to *His Nature*, but He also works with us according to what He knows of *our nature*. Which is more than we know.

During that first dark period of which I wrote in *The Burden Is Light*, I did give up every conscious right to myself. I was sincere. Great release came. And after it, came several years of fairly smooth going. Then, when God saw it was time to show me more dust in the depths of my personality which needed to be cleansed and given over to Him, He permitted certain situations to arise in my life which pointed them out to me glaringly. At first, I was depressed. Then again, seeing much more than I had been able to see before, there was another time of reckoning. There have been others since. There will be more. But for the past three years, I have been free of the accompanying depression and discouragement, because He has taught me not only more of what is in my human nature, but more of what is in His God Nature.

I am His responsibility entirely now. But by no means do I intend to infer that I am an advanced Christian. I am still a sinner who not only must, but joyfully *can* come to Him at any time and hand back the reins of the wild horses of her personality.

We dare not rely for one moment on one or one hundred "spiritual experiences." But for every moment of all the years of our earthly lives and throughout an endless eternity, we can rely on the living Person of Jesus Christ. And we can do this because of what He is like.

So much of the confusion among all Christians, new and not so new, could be wiped out if we were all really growing "in the knowledge of Jesus Christ." I can't grow spiritually. Neither can you. But my spiritual growth occurs, I find, in direct proportion to the increase of my knowledge of Him. No one will ever be willing to place her life in the hands of a stranger. If you are hesitating on this point, follow His simple advice to you: "Learn of me. . . ." Once you have learned of Him, you will want to belong to Him. And once He is in control of your life, you will find yourself more eager than ever to learn still more of what Jesus Christ is really like. And when you know the Nature of Jesus Christ, you know the Nature of God.

17

The Difference Christ Makes . . .

IN THE WAY YOU FACE LIFE

17

The Difference Christ Makes...

IN THE WAY YOU FACE LIFE

I am writing this book during the time of year when
Chicago is thawing its foggy, dark way out of a tussle with
an unusual winter onslaught. For weeks, people have been
late for work. For weeks, the hospitals have been crowded
with casualties ranging from broken elbows, to broken legs,
to sprained backs, to cracked skulls. The side-streets in the
neighborhood sections are still rough as country roads with
dirty, deep furrows of old ice. The snow has stopped, but the
black water pools itself dangerously over hidden ice-cakes
and people are still slipping and still falling and still crowding the hospitals. Still getting their pictures in the paper,
replete with crutches and slings, and captioned by the warn-
ing that citizens are to be careful because they are of more
use to their employers late for work than laid up in bed
for weeks.

I spent three and one-half hours at the hairdresser's yesterday getting a permanent, and I listened steadily to three
and one-half hours of stories and complaints about the
weather from the other women who were also there.

As each woman told her special series of stories about how winter had mistreated her, I was aware of one unbroken theme: Winter has no right to treat *me* this way! One of these stories will show you what I mean.

"I tell you, I've had it! I never want to live through another winter like this one. It's all right for these women with husbands to handle things like frozen cars. But I'm alone in the world. When I go I have to get there myself. One morning, I remember, I pried and chiseled and pried at that car door and finally I walked three blocks—three blocks, mind you—in below zero weather to a filling station where I always have my car serviced. And do you think one of those lazy fellows would take time to come and help me? Not on your sweet life. The most they would do for me was to charge me twenty cents for a little old plastic snow scraper, the kind they used to give away for advertising purposes! Oh, yes, I finally got it open. Then, when I got to work, the first thing I did was break my key chain. But I got all the keys picked up—I thought. All day long everything went wrong. That night I tried to start my car. Dead battery. Dead as a doornail. And do you think I could get any no-good garage man to come and fix it? Not for two hours! Two hours, mind you. Well, when I got home at 9:30 at night, I was fit to be tied. I took out my key chain and what do you think! I'd managed to pick up all the keys that morning when I broke the chain—except—*except* my front door key! My daughter was out, of course. Teenagers always are. And I'll have you know I sat in my car and waited for two solid hours until she finally got home. I took one look at her and said, 'Don't say one word to me. Don't even say hello. I'm in no shape to talk. Just go to your own room and I'll go to mine. I'm fit to be tied.' She did and I did. I thought I'd never get warm. Oh, I tell you, I've had it. I've had it."

The filling station boys and the garage mechanics had no right to be busy when this woman needed them. Her house key had deliberately jumped off that broken key chain. Of all the keys on the chain, it had the least right to be so inconsiderate. And above all, her daughter had no right whatever to come in late to open the door for her mother.

I do not blame this woman for feeling frustrated. I do not blame her one bit for her self-pity. Not for one moment do I underestimate the pressure that particular day put on her human nature. I have merely used it as an illustration to strengthen our theme concerning the difference it makes whether or not a woman's personality is Christ-controlled.

It is often much easier to be brave and courageous and calm in the face of great tragedy than it is to remain poised and quiet in the face of life's small irritations. And this woman (if the remainder of her conversation was an indication, and I think it was), was not a believer in Jesus Christ. She was a sincere, hard-working woman. But daily life, if it veered from the normal in any way, was simply too much for her. She had nothing with which to meet it.

A few days ago, I received a letter from a good friend which further illustrates my point. She, too, is a working gal. Her letter, in contrast to the above narration of steady complaint, was one of the most hilarious I have ever read! A flat tire, a stalled battery, also a lost key, a traffic ticket, a hectic day of suffering patients in and out of the doctor's office where she works, a temper display by the doctor, all woven together in a letter of praise to prove that even daily life can be coped with, if Christ is in control of the personality. Her letter ended this way: "A few years ago, I'd be frantically calling people on the telephone right now, to tell my sad tale about 'my day.' Instead, I thought I'd just write to you and tell you that 'the Lord is risen!' The first thing that happened rocked me. But I decided to do as you once told me we could do. I decided to let every other thing that might happen that day be a *reminder* that Christ lived in me and that He has real humor and real poise and can handle anything that comes along. Do you know something, old girl? You're right! He can and He does. I love Him more than ever. This day which could have been a nerve-wrecker has been better than a whole week at a Bible conference."

Life, however, is much more than flat tires and lost keys and the seemingly small irritations that pelt us all now and then. Life is made up of our thoughts, our actions, our temptations, our troubles. A widow wrote: "My social security is not enough to live on and I have just lost the part-time job I had. I'm not strong physically and I'm too old for most people to hire. I'm desperate. Could you help me find a job? I've somehow lost my closeness to God. I'm really desperate."

When I receive letters like this, I sometimes have to stop everything and remember that the Lord told us to roll everything off onto Him. I become so burdened with these real and heartbreaking problems that depression is hard to resist. Of course, I have no concrete way of helping. I wish I had, but I haven't. And during these times, I am held steady by the sure knowledge that He cares more about these people than I could ever care. Because He is Love. In the case of this woman, I wrote as clearly and as firmly as I could, that even though she had lost touch with God, she could be absolutely sure that God had not lost touch with her. It is difficult to be firm with a woman in such a desperate state of mind. But in all honesty, I had to remind her that her life (from her side of things) was not Christ-controlled. It was desperation-controlled. I reminded her that Paul wrote in the fourth chapter of his second letter to the Corinthian Christians, that "We are troubled on every side, yet not distressed; we are perplexed, but not in despair;

persecuted, but not forsaken; cast down, but not destroyed; always bearing about in the body the dying of the Lord Jesus, that the life also of Jesus might be made manifest in our body."

This is not an admonition. It is a fact. Paul is stating, from his own experience, what he knows to be possible for all Christ-controlled personalities.

Just yesterday (as I write this chapter) another letter came from another widow. "Dear Genie, My testing time seems to be increasing in intensity. I had just found a nice small apartment for my little boy and myself upstairs in the house of a lovely family. I also liked my work in a bookstore. Then, on Monday (the day after I found a wonderful little church with a marvelous minister who seems to care), I was taken home from work very, very ill. My doctor put me to bed and called my boss at the bookstore and told him it was either my heart, pleurisy, or gall bladder. But he told him he thought I could be back in one week. Genie, less than thirty minutes later my boss called the hospital and said business was slack and as I was the last person hired, he would have to lay me off permanently. Here I lie in the hospital with no job, ill, and almost a complete stranger in this big city. On top of this, the next day my dear friend downstairs told me she was moving out. But, Christ is with me. I know I am not alone. And He showed His love today when the little minister whose church I had only attended once, came to visit me. He is so kind and so gentle and so Christ-like. I am not brave. I am very scared and worried. But I am determined to *know* that Christ is with me and loves me, even when I do not feel His love. With no job, ill in a hospital and no place to go when I get out, I am having a glorious chance to try Him!"

Here again, is proof that even though we suffer and are sometimes afraid, it makes all the difference between despair and hope, when we *determine* to remember who He is and what He is like.

The strengthening Presence of Jesus Christ in the aspects of life which shock society, may not be of personal interest to most of you. But it will be to some. Wrong relationships such as adultery are part of life.

Here are excerpts from two letters.

"Dear Genie Price, At nineteen I married a fine Christian man. We were going to serve God together. But it didn't work out that way. What kind of a Christian life can you have if you don't read the Bible and pray together? We haven't. And now, I am more miserable than I can put into words.

"From being told practically every day that I am too fat and that nothing I ever do is right; from being pushed off when I want to kiss my husband; from being 'talked down to' constantly, I am now strongly attracted to another man.

"How do these things start? I used to 'look down' on any person who committed adultery, wondering just how they could ever do such a thing! Believe me, from now on, I shall have nothing but compassion for them.

"Just the very act of caring that I had a splitting headache, started it. This man was sympathetic. My husband always told me to stop pretending I had one. I can talk to this man in a way I could never talk to my husband. But, Genie, I don't want to be involved like this. How can I get back into fellowship with Christ?"

This woman answered her own question without realizing it. "What kind of Christian life can you have if you don't read the Bible and pray together?" I urged her to begin showing kindness and interest toward her husband whether she felt like it or not. And above all, to begin to spend time alone with the Lord. He is Love. He understands her predicament completely and He is *not shocked*. He knew this affair was going to happen when He saved this woman. And He knows the way out of it. Of course, she will have to be willing to stop seeing the other man. I advised her to do this and to fill the emptiness with time spent with the Lord alone and also to ask Him to send someone to her with whom she can pray. When we remain alone where our thoughts rule us, we only get mired more deeply into wrong relationships. Coming out of a situation like this is not easy. It is painful and it is heartbreaking. But the Lord knows this, too. And He is right in it with us. Some definite action on our part, however, is necessary. We must decide to spend time with Him. We must decide to show kindness and concern for the person with whom God has placed us. God is Love and He can rekindle love. Perhaps most important of all, on the part of a woman involved in this way, is to pray with a small group of other women. She doesn't need to bare her soul to them. But she will be strengthened by honest prayer with other women.

This is certainly borne out in part of the next letter I want to share with you. "Dear Genie, how can I ever tell you of the joy in my heart. I can look at my kids now and feel clean! I can't say I'm in love with their father yet, but I'm on my way. And I know I would never have been able to break off this affair if I had not given over all the controls of my life to Jesus. I figure it this way. If He says adultery is a sin and if He died to break the dominion of sin in my life, then He just has to have a practical way out for me. Hooray! He has. Don't think I'm not still tempted. But I have found myself becoming more and more interested in reading the Bible now. I'm not fighting God any longer. And even though some of the members of my little prayer group don't know any of this, I keep trying to thank them just for meeting together! It has been a real, concrete help to me to have these little informal, honest sessions with the other gals. I've discovered I'm not the only sinner in the world and not the only woman with a mess of problems. Every time I hear my husband come in the house at night, I quickly turn to the Lord and ask Him to give me His love for him and to help me think of some little way to show this love. And, even though sometimes it seems awfully slow to me, it's working. P.S. Of course, I'm not seeing the other fellow anymore at all."

It has been said that there are some problems which we cannot untangle. We must cut them off. But the strain of the sudden severing is too much for the fiber of the human personality to withstand unless the emptiness is filled with something new. This woman wisely became a part of a living prayer cell. She put herself deliberately in a place of vital contact with Christ Himself. Of course, there was suffering, but she found Him in it with her.

The nature of the problem which is tangling your life is not the point. The point is the Nature of Christ. But we are usually not willing to let Him have His own lovely way in our involvements *until* we have taken an honest look at our own natures.

Do you realize that you, and the "self" which is the accumulated image of the years of your life, are two separate things? But the real *you* is capable of judging that second "self" which your life has molded and shaped. You may even hate that "self" you see as you stand by and watch. But how few have a true picture of it? Your second "self" has a body-image which is no doubt radically different from the figure you see in your mirror. Your second "self" also has a personality-image which is just as different. Most of us dislike a three-way mirror in a dress shop. It shows us from angles we don't often see. But that three-way look can whip us up to do something about our bodies, just as an all around look at our personalities can do.

Many women dress as though they were a svelte twenty-one, when actually they are a well-padded fifty. The same analogy covers our self-image. With the years, we build up these extra images of ourselves and they are powerful. Powerful to blind us to our real needs. If you are a hefty middle-aged woman with an exalted opinion of her own righteousness, God can do no more to correct your personality than a billowy skirt can do to correct your waistline! We must deal with ourselves as we are. That is the way God deals with us.

If we feel inferior, we react with hostility and anxiety when we meet new people. We are sure they won't like us. If we feel superior, we also react with hostility, since we are quite sure no one will really appreciate our golden selves. Your parents helped form your self-image. The circumstances of your life helped form it. And you, unconsciously, have done your part, too.

An accepted way to begin to see yourself as you really are is to write down the names of all the persons who have exerted a strong influence on your life. Try to understand why and what. Ask the Holy Spirit to bring circumstances to your mind which have seemingly forced you into your present pattern. He will be right in it with you. He will give you courage to take a direct, unveiled look at you as you are.

Another excellent method of self-detection is to check yourself under varying circumstances at the end of a day. Ask yourself questions like: Do I always have to be inconspicuous? Do I always have to be conspicuous? Am I comfortable only when I am thought modest? Do I have to see to it that I waste no time? Am I compelled to stay busy? Do I have to feel that everyone likes me? Do I look for sympathy? Do I seek praise for my deeds well done? Do I press for praise when it doesn't come? Do I panic when I serve an inferior dish at dinner before guests? Can I forget unpleasant events, or do I chew them over and over? Can I take constructive criticism? Do I defend myself?

You may enlarge the list.

Another way to discover your hidden self is to make a list of your basic assumptions about life. Ideas such as the fact that mothers should always love their children. That women need special protection and care. That illness entitles a person to much sympathy. That people just should not commit social sins. That other persons should act and react according to what you believe to be right. The point is not whether these attitudes are true or false, but checking your own assumptions against them will most likely reveal hostile areas in your hidden nature. You can then bring these hostilities directly to Jesus Christ and together you can work them out. You can follow Jesus Christ in His personal integrity.

Dr. Samuel Shoemaker wrote: "It is not that we are either great sinners or great saints. It is that we fluctuate and vacillate from one to the other. Integrity consists, in part, of exploding any notion that we are either irremediable sinners, or saints with no need for improvement; and of accepting simply the fact that we are just such vacillating people, always needing the forgiveness and grace of God.

"Christianity is not a side light shining from the periphery of life; Christianity is a revealed insight from out of the very heart of life itself. Perhaps there is no surer test for our real integrity than what we do with the insights which we discover in Christianity. If we head right into them, and let them reveal ourselves to us, we shall have integrity. If we reject or evade them, we shall have the dividedness of mind which is dishonest at the start, and becomes more neurotic as time goes on."

If we form the habit of remembering that we cannot get out of the Presence of God, we will be quick to see the false image of ourselves which life has built around us. We may not be entirely to blame for the falseness of this image, but if we know Christ, we are to blame if nothing is done to clear it up. Many, many women are entirely too introspective. This is a subtle form of self-love. But now and then we need to take an honest look at what we think we are. And under the direction of the Holy Spirit and with our Bibles open at some psychologically searching passage such as the Sermon on the Mount or the thirteenth chapter of First Corinthians, take a good clear look. What you see may sicken you. That's all right. No time need elapse between the look and repentance and release. Jesus Christ did a complete thing on Calvary. And you not only have the act of Calvary on which to rely, you have the One who hung there right beside you to help you correct what you find.

Life is too hard to cope with alone. Surely, there is no need to remind you by now, that you will be adequate to face life only if Jesus Christ is in control of your personality.

18

The Difference Christ Makes . . .

IN THE WAY YOU

FACE DEATH

18

The Difference Christ Makes...

IN THE WAY YOU FACE DEATH

"Dear Genie Price, I have a wonderful story of God's Love to tell you. I had just returned from the doctor's office where I had learned that I was two months pregnant. My heart was so heavy. I already had five healthy children and wondered why this had happened. I wasn't ready to face another ordeal such as childbirth has been for me. Then about seven o'clock that same day, my sister called to say my father had passed away. . . . A few months later, my husband's father died of a brain tumor. In the meantime my mother had been hospitalized with a kidney infection. She had expected to go home on Wednesday, but grew worse, underwent surgery and died in just three weeks. My mother and father and my father-in-law all three in such a short time. But honestly, I feel as though I have just been converted! God has been so good and has taught me many new ways to lay hold of His grace. I suppose we never really learn until we are forced to. Although this has been a heartbreaking time, I thank God for all of it. I just wanted to share this great experience of His Love with you. Surely, Jesus is Lord!"

"Dear Genie, It's Christmas Day and for the first time in three years I am glad it is Christmas Day. For me, it is deep with the reality of Christ. Nothing can ever, ever shake me from the belief that it *was* God who was born in that old rough manger that first Christmas. I know it was God because only God could put joy back into Christmas for me! I know you know about my mother's death, but somehow I've never been able to tell you that she committed suicide on Christmas Day. My darling mother, whom I loved so much. And for whom life was just too heavy to carry around any more. I've fought God every inch of the way. Why did she have to leap from a bridge into that icy river on Christmas Day? I screamed my question at Him over and over, but now that my own life is linked to the Life of Christ, He has quieted my questioning with His Love. I can leave all things in His dear hands and know that all is well somehow. I don't understand any more than I did, but I don't fight to understand any more. Learning something of what He is really like has quieted my heart and my mind. I am loving all of life this Christmas Day and that is surely a miracle of Love."

"O death, where is thy sting? O grave, where is thy victory?. . . Thanks be to God which giveth us the victory through our Lord Jesus Christ."

How? How does God give a victory when the house is so empty? How does God give a victory when we have wept so much that any more tears will *have* to come from our broken hearts? Isn't there a new, cruel sting every morning when sleep fades and realization lashes at us all over again? Hasn't the grave won? Isn't all that we loved of that beloved one lying there under the ground?

"Thanks be to God which giveth us the victory through our Lord Jesus Christ."

How does He do it? Words become stubborn, useless

things when we try to explain. But to the hearts of those among us who have lost loved ones by death, there is a deep knowing that He does. We still weep. But that's all right. "Jesus wept." The house is still empty. The family still has to talk a lot more and try to think of funny things to say in order to keep everyone's mind off the empty place at the table. Or perhaps you are a widow, who, like my own mother, sits alone at your table.

While the arrangements were still going on and the calls from friends were still coming in, the loneliness didn't fall on you so sharply. But now, when you come out to the kitchen in the morning there isn't anyone to speak to. Your life seems lived up against a high wall. You can't even shout over it.

How is the sting gone and the victory realized? Paul says it is "through Jesus Christ our Lord."

It is. If your grief is fresh, or if it is old, stop now and realize in detail that on every point, in all of your sorrow, Jesus Christ has identified with you. He was called "a man of sorrows and acquainted with grief." Your grief is no strange thing to Him. "Surely he hath borne our griefs and carried our sorrows." Surely He is bearing yours now.

Are these pious platitudes? Suitable verses to use on sympathy cards? No. These are facts. But there are certain things which we must do before they become accessible to us.

First of all, we must spend enough time in learning what Jesus Christ is really like, so that we are willing to let go of our questioning. No one has a complete answer to the why of human suffering. Because He knows where He is moving with His creation, for reasons of His own, God permits both sin and suffering. It has been said that a scarlet thread runs throughout the pattern of the whole universe. "The lamb was slain before the foundation of the world." In one sense

Calvary has always been. In every sense it will always be. And right here, as we face either the present reality or the future possibility of losing our loved ones in death, we must take hold of the fact that Christ Himself demonstrated on the Cross that *nothing* ever needs to be wasted if He is on the scene.

But as long as we block Him with our whys, we have not realized that as He hung on the Cross, He made provision for release from bitterness and anguish as well as release from the dominion of sin. Jesus Christ has already asked why for us! To you as women, I dare to plead that you will prepare yourself for what comes to us all eventually. For several years I have been urging acceptance of the human suffering from which none of us is immune. It will come to us all. To face this fact is not being morbid. It is merely being realistic. And unless you have sufficiently acquainted yourself with the true Nature of Jesus Christ before death slashes across your personal life, you can easily go down under its slashing. There is no other way to prepare for it. Jesus urged us to learn of Him. That is the secret. He will not wave a wand over you and dissipate your grief. But you will be permitted to enter into a new kind of intimacy with Him, when your loved one is gone. Somehow, we don't enter into this intimacy until we are forced to do it. But the door is always open for our entering. My mother, so recently widowed, urges me to tell you to stop every sudden swamp of grief with prayer. She wrote: "There have been evenings when I have gone to my knees three times as I made my way back to the bedroom alone! Always by the time I got there, I knew the Lord was with me."

We are given the victory "*through* our Lord Jesus Christ." He Himself, when His own heart was heavy with grief at the death of His beloved cousin and friend, John the Baptist, tried to get away alone. This is the human tendency. We long to shut ourselves up and treasure what we have lost. During our own suffering we must never forget that Jesus was human, too. "When Jesus heard of it (the death of John the Baptist), he departed thence by ship into a desert place apart: and when the people heard thereof, they followed him on foot out of the cities. And Jesus went forth, and saw a great multitude, and was moved with compassion toward them, and he healed their sick." Jesus longed to get away, to shut himself up and grieve for John. He understands your tendency to do the same thing. *But* "they followed Him." He was not permitted the luxury of privacy even at such a time. He was followed by multitudes of people dragging the load of their own need. Did He demand His right to suffer in privacy? No. And here is the creative lesson for us in our times of sorrow. "Jesus went forth. . . ." He knew of the need and He "went forth . . . and was moved with compassion toward them, and he healed their sick."

You are needed, too, somewhere, by someone. Perhaps by many. Jesus did not act as He did merely to give us something difficult to live up to. He acted as He did because He had created human nature and knew what would heal it! This brought not only healing to the multitudes who received His touch, it brought healing to His own grieving heart, too.

It won't take long to find those who need you. But you must stir yourself up and "go forth." You may not want to do it. Understandably you will want privacy. But the same life which moved Jesus of Nazareth will move you, if you are movable.

And always we must remember that our loved ones are not really dead. I was gloriously aware of this as I looked at my father in his coffin last summer. I saw only a bad photograph of his real living self! One way in which this fact of eternal living has been brought home to me is to realize that my essential self feels now at forty-two just the same as she did as a child. The essential self of our loved ones does not even lose consciousness. I read this once in an old book by Dwight L. Moody and I believe it with all my heart. Perhaps we are somewhat pagan to attend to the bodies of our loved ones whose essential selves have only been released so that they can really live.

The years may seem to stretch endlessly ahead for us. But once more, we must stir ourselves up to remember that God is dwelling along with our loved ones in an Eternal Now. And because we have received Eternal Life when we received Christ, we, too dwell in that same Eternal Now. It does not stretch out like a ribbon as time does. It surrounds us and dwells within us and we dwell within it.

A friend of mine asked an electronics expert to compute for her an average life span on earth, on the basis of the Bible's statement that a day is as a thousand years to the Lord. She wanted to know how long our lifetime really is to God, in relation to eternity. The answer came back: The average human life span is about one hour and fifteen minutes! I remarked to Mother one day not long ago that Dad must be restless for us to get there too, since he had always hated to wait. Mother smiled and said, "I suppose he realizes I only have about fifteen minutes more, and then I'll be there, too."

We can face our own deaths, too, "through our Lord Jesus Christ." There is no other way to face them. Once more, He has identified with us here. He died also. And then He came back to reassure us that it is all right, all the way there and back.

Life is going on for our loved ones and it will go on for us in an atmosphere of freedom which we cannot begin to comprehend in our mortal bodies. Jesus Christ took the victory away from the grave and gave it to us.

The deep responsibility of being women is brought sharply into focus where death is concerned. Did Jesus have a deep, important motive in making His great statement about Eternal Life to Martha, a woman? I believe He did. After all, He, above anyone else in the world knew the tremendous power of a woman's life to mark other lives. And so, "Jesus said to *her*, I am the resurrection, and the life: he that believeth in me, though he were dead, yet shall he live: and whosoever liveth and believeth in me shall never die."

My mother's faith in this statement of Jesus is marking my life with joy and lightening my burden these days. She could be marking it another way.

You, just by being a woman, are marking lives, too. As I am. As are all women everywhere in the world.

Do we leave the gentle, creative marks of the Lord Jesus? Or do we leave the scars of our own self-centered lives?

If Christ lives in us, controlling our personalities, we will leave glorious marks on the lives we touch. Not because of our lovely characters, but because of His.

CPSIA information can be obtained
at www.ICGtesting.com
Printed in the USA
JSHW031223271220
10553JS00001BA/2